TOP 10
ATHENS

CORAL DAVENPORT
JANE FOSTER

EYEWITNESS TRAVEL

Left **Temple of Hephaestus, Agora** Centre **Glass bottle, Benaki Museum** Right **Kapnikarea**

LONDON, NEW YORK,
MELBOURNE, MUNICH AND DELHI
www.dk.com

Produced by Blue Island Publishing
Reproduced by Colourscan, Singapore
Printed and bound in China by Leo
Paper Products Ltd

First published in Great Britain in 2004
by Dorling Kindersley Limited
80 Strand, London WC2R 0RL
A Penguin Company

A CIP catalogue record is available from
the British Library.

ISBN: 978-1-40532-774-9

Within each Top 10 list in this book, no
hierarchy of quality or popularity is
implied. All 10 are, in the editor's
opinion, of roughly equal merit.

Contents

Athens' Top 10

Cover: Front – **DK Images**: Rob Reichenfeld bl; **Alamy Images**: © nagelestock.com main image;
Maria Stefossi: clb. Spine – **DK Images**: Nigel Hicks. Back – **DK Images**: Joe Cornish tc; Rob Reichenfeld tl, tr.

Left **Greek soldiers** Centre **Island of Aegina** Right **Souvlaki restaurants, Monastiraki**

Left **Herodes Atticus Theatre** Right **View of the Peloponnese and Poros town**

 Key to abbreviations
Adm *admission charge payable* **A/C** *air conditioning*

ATHENS'
TOP 10

ATHENS' TOP 10

🔟 Highlights of Athens

Athens is simultaneously known as the Classical, marble-pillared cradle of Western civilization and as a modern urban sprawl of concrete and traffic. Between the extremes lies a kaleidoscopic city, where the in- fluences of East and West entwine in the markets, cafés and tavernas, built upon ancient ruins and rubbing shoulders with gold-leafed Byzantine churches.

Tower of the Winds detail

Acropolis
The crown jewel of Greece, if not all of Europe. Its temples are the most influential buildings in Western architecture. *(See pp8–11.)*

The Agora
Socrates, Aristotle and St Paul all held forth in the market- place below the Acropolis. This was the heart of the ancient city. *(See pp12–15.)*

National Archaeo- logical Museum
The greatest collection of finds from some of the world's greatest cultures is housed here *(above)*. Exhibits include the gold treasure of Mycenae and the first sculptures to depict the complexity of the human form. *(See pp16–17.)*

Museum of Cycladic Art
The world's largest collection of Cycladic art showcases a matriarchal island culture whose 5,000-year-old icons still inspire artists of the modern world. *(See pp18–19.)*

Vathis

Kerameikos

Psiri

Thissio

Agora ②

Monastiraki

Anafiotika

Acropolis ①

Hill of the Nymphs

Filopappos Hill ⑨

Makrigianni

Omonia

5 Roman Forum and Tower of the Winds

The Romans abandoned the ancient Agora and created this orderly new commercial centre. Its showpiece was the magnificent Tower of the Winds, which housed an ingenious water clock. (See pp20–21.)

6 Benaki Museum

A first-rate collection of Greek art from Neolithic to present times. It is housed in a beautifully renovated Neo-Classical mansion (left), with an intriguing history and famed rooftop view. (See pp22–23.)

7 Kerameikos

Classical Athens' cemetery gives a fascinating cross-section of life, and death, at the city's edge, with elaborate tombs (above), temples, sacred roads – and an ancient brothel. (See pp26–7.)

AFTOKRATOROS IRAKLEIOU
3
Areos
Strefi Hill
KALIDROMIOU
TRIKOUPI
Exarcheia
CHARILAOU
IPPOKRATOUS
AKADIMIAS
Neapoli
Lykavittos Hill
PLATEIA LYKAVITTOU
STADIOU
PANEPISTIMIOU
ALKAS MAS
SKOUFA
Kolonaki
PLATEIA IFTHIMONOS
PLATEIA DEXAMENI
PLATEIA KOLONAKI
Syntagma
ELEFTHERIOU VENIZELOU (V. SOFIAS)
6 **4**
8
ERMOU
ITROPOLEOS
PLATEIA SYNTAGMA
FILELLINON
LEOFOROS VASILISSIS AMALIAS
National Gardens
LEOFOROS V.
LEOFOROS VASILEOS KONSTANTINOU GEORGIOU B
IRODOU
Plaka
PLATEIA IL DIMOUSOU
LATEIA KRATOUS
LEOF VASILISSIS OLGAS
Zappeion Gardens
10
PLATEIA STADIOU
ERATOSTHENOUS
ATHAN. DIAKOU
ARDITTOU
PLATEIA PLASTIRA
500 ⌐ yards ⌐0⌐ metres ⌐ 500

8 Byzantine Museum

The rich, complex history of the Byzantine Empire is told through the greatest of its works, from the intricacy of precious metalwork to the solemnity of the many icons. (See pp28–9.)

9 Filopappos Hill

A green-gladed respite in the city centre, with a wonderful view and a mix of monuments that encompass ancient (left), Byzantine and modern Greek culture. (See pp30–31.)

10 Temple of Olympian Zeus

Ancient Greece's most colossal temple (above) stands beside the monumental arch that divided Athens between Greek hero Theseus and formidable Roman emperor Hadrian. (See pp32–33.)

TOP 10 Acropolis

The temples on the "Sacred Rock" of Athens are considered the most important monuments in the Western world, for they have exerted more influence on our architecture than anything since. The great marble masterpieces were constructed during the late 5th-century BC reign of Perikles, the Golden Age of Athens. Most were temples built to honour Athena, the city's patron goddess. Still breathtaking for their proportion and scale, both human and majestic, the temples were adorned with magnificent, dramatic sculptures of the gods.

Acropolis from the rocky outcrop of Areopagos

🕐 Visit first thing in the morning or at sunset to avoid the energy-sapping midday heat and multitudinous tour groups.

🍴 The cantinas at the Acropolis are outrageously overpriced. Bring your own (large) bottle of water and a snack.

- Map J4
- 210 321 4172-2
- www.culture.gr
- Metro: Akropoli
- Apr–Sep: 8am–7pm daily; Oct–Mar: 8:30am–3pm daily
- Adm €12; students half price
- Admission price includes entry into Kerameikos, Theatre of Dionysus, Agora, Roman Forum and Temple of Olympian Zeus (valid for 4 days)

Top 10 Sights

1. Acropolis Rock
2. Propylaia
3. Temple of Athena Nike
4. Panathenaic Way
5. Parthenon
6. Erechtheion
7. Acropolis Museum
8. Panagia Chrysospiliotissa
9. Herodes Atticus Theatre
10. Dionysus Theatre

Acropolis Rock 1

As the highest part of the city, the rock is an ideal place for refuge, religion and royalty. The Acropolis Rock has been used continuously for these purposes since Neolithic times.

Propylaia 2

At the top of the rock, you are greeted by the Propylaia *(above)*, the grand entrance through which all visitors passed to reach the summit temples.

Temple of Athena Nike ("Victory") 3

There has been a temple to a goddess of victory at this location since prehistoric times, as it protects and stands over the part of the rock most vulnerable to enemy attack.

Panathenaic Way 4

The route used in an ancient procession when a new tunic, or *peplos*, would have been offered to Athena, along with sacrifices.

Parthenon 5

This was the epitome of ancient Greek Classical art, a magnificent "Temple to the Virgin", goddess Athena, who was represented inside by a giant gold and ivory sculpture.

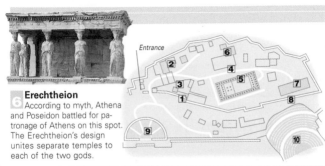

Erechtheion

According to myth, Athena and Poseidon battled for patronage of Athens on this spot. The Erechtheion's design unites separate temples to each of the two gods.

Entrance

Acropolis Museum

The current museum is to be superseded by the glittering New Acropolis Museum, opening in early 2008 *(see pp10–11)*, but for a while they will both be in operation.

Panagia Chrysospiliotissa

Originally dedicated to the god of wine and revelry, the cave was later turned into the church of the Virgin of the Golden Cave.

Herodes Atticus Theatre

A much later addition *(right)*, built in 161 by its namesake. In summer it hosts the Athens Festival *(see pp60–61)*.

Dionysus Theatre

This mosaic-tiled theatre was the site of Classical Greece's drama competitions, where the tragedies and comedies by the great playwrights (Aeschylus, Sophocles, Euripides) were first performed. The theatre seated 15,000, and you can still see engraved front-row marble seats, reserved for priests of Dionysus.

The Acropolis in Later Times

In the 5th century AD, the Parthenon was used as a church. During the Ottoman occupation, it was used as a mosque, and the Erechtheion as a harem. The Ottomans also kept gunpowder in the Parthenon, which led to its near destruction when the Venetians shelled it during the siege of 1687 *(see p31)*. The Parthenon suffered further damage in 1799 when Lord Elgin removed sculptures, taking them back to England. The current restoration will finish in 2008.

Left and Right **Sculptures from the ancient temples**

TOP 10 New Acropolis Museum

1 The Glass Floor
The museum is built directly over an early Christian settlement. Glass floors will allow visitors to look directly down into the site while surrounded by Classical and Archaic sculptures.

2 The Parthenon Marbles
The marbles will be displayed in the order in which they would have graced the Parthenon, with blank spaces significantly left for sculptures that remain in London.

3 The Calf-Bearer
This joyous Archaic sculpture shows a bearded man carrying a calf, to be offered as a sacrifice to Athena. The statue itself was a votive offering and dates to 570 BC.

4 The Peplos Kore
One of the most exquisite of the Archaic votive statues. Her gown, called a *peplos*, was painted with decorative colours. Traces of paint are still visible on her eyes, lips and curly hair.

5 Kore with Almond-Shaped Eyes
The most sumptuous of the votive *koroi* – her detailed drapery and fully formed body show real development in sculpture. Her dress was painted with detailed patterns, including a

The Calf-Bearer

border with the distinctive "Greek key" pattern.

6 Pediment of the Ancient Temple
Part of the pediment of an ancient temple to Athena, built before the Parthenon and later destroyed, shows Athena fighting against a Giant. It dates to 520 BC.

7 The Kritios Boy
This beautiful sculpture of a young male athlete marks the transition from Archaic to early Classical sculpture, with the introduction of a naturalistic pose. The Kritos Boy sculpture dates to 480 BC.

8 Relief of the "Mourning Athena"
This tiny relief shows the goddess Athena as a girl, without sword or shield and clad in an Attic *peplos*.

9 The Caryatids
The original statued pillars that supported the Erechtheion's porch have been brought inside for protection. Their arms are broken now, but initially they held libation bowls.

10 Frieze on the Temple of Athena Nike
The small but dynamically sculpted frieze shows scenes of battle, with gods, Persians and Greeks all stepping into the fray.

For an explanation of artistic styles and terms **see pp42–3**

Top 10 Scenes Depicted in the Parthenon Marbles

1. The birth of Athena, springing fully formed out of Zeus's head *(see p38)*
2. The Pantheon watching Athena's birth
3. Athena and Poseidon's fight for control of the city *(see p38)*
4. The gods watch and take sides in Athena and Poseidon's battle
5. The Panathenaic Procession, ancient Athens' most important religious event
6. The battle of the Centaurs and Lapiths
7. The battle of the gods and the Giants
8. The battle of the Greeks and the Amazons
9. The sack of Troy
10. Priestesses prepare a veil for Athena

More than a Building

Old Acropolis Museum

The small, worn-around-the edges Acropolis Museum had never really done justice to the stunning treasures it held within. But the Greek government's multi-storey, all-glass showpiece of a new museum at the foot of the Acropolis does. Most of the old museum's contents are scheduled to be moved to the new museum when it opens in early 2008. However, there's an ulterior motive to the construction of this new museum, which is to send a pointed international message. In 1799, the seventh Earl of Elgin cut off two-thirds of the sculptures of gods, men and monsters adorning the Parthenon and took them to England. Most were sold to the British Museum, which refuses to return them, saying Athens cannot display them adequately or safely. Now, in turn, Athens can reply that the new museum answers this criticism and eliminates the last barrier to returning the marbles, for which a special room awaits in the new museum. Greece hopes that when thousands of international visitors see the sparkling but empty showcase, it will ratchet up the pressure on Britain, forcing a much-anticipated return of the marbles.

Artist's impression of the New Acropolis Museum

New Acropolis Museum
Glass walls will allow a direct view of the Acropolis temples from within the museum, while the glass floor will give a view over the ruins of an early Christian settlement.

The Parthenon will be directly visible through the museum's glass walls

Note: The New Acropolis Museum is located in Makrigianni – at K6 on the Central Athens map on the back flap

TOP 10 The Agora

Athens' ancient marketplace, founded in the 6th century BC, was the heart of the city for 1,200 years. It was the centre for all civic activities, including politics, commerce, philosophy, religion, arts and athletics. This is where Socrates addressed his public, where democracy was born and where St Paul preached. Because of its varied uses, the rambling site can be confusing. But, unlike the sweltering Acropolis, the grassy Agora is a great place to wander, imagining the lively bustle that once filled this historic centre.

Odeon of Agrippa

Top 10 Sights

1. Stoa Basileios
2. Odeon of Agrippa
3. Temple of Hephaestus
4. Tholos
5. Great Drain
6. Monument of the Eponymous Heroes
7. Altar of Zeus Agoraios
8. Middle Stoa
9. Nymphaion
10. Stoa of Attalos

Statues in front of the Odeon of Agrippa

The best overview of the Agora is from the Areopagos rock (see p53).

Most places surrounding the Agora serve tourist fare; Athenians however head for To Kouti on Adrianou for twists on taverna classics. Try the rose-petal ice cream!

• Adrianou, Monastiraki
• Map B4
• Metro: Monastiraki
• 210 321 0185
• www.culture.gr
• Mar–Dec: 8am–7:30pm daily; Jan & Feb: 8:30am–3pm daily
• Adm €4, or included with Acropolis ticket

Stoa Basileios

Built in 500 BC, this building housed the office of legal affairs concerning ancient cults. Most of it was destroyed when the Goths invaded Athens in AD267. Its ruins are best viewed from Adrianou.

Odeon of Agrippa

Marcus Vipsanius Agrippa, an official with the first emperor Augustus, had this theatre built in AD 15. Outside stood statues featuring three serpent-tailed Giants and Tritons on huge plinths. Two Tritons and a Giant still remain.

Temple of Hephaestus

Temple of Hephaestus

The best-preserved Classical temple in Greece, devoted jointly to Hephaestus and Athena. Its fantastical frieze depicts the deeds of Theseus and Herakles.

Tholos

The 50-member executive committee of the first parliament lived and worked in this circular building, whose name translates as "beehive".

Great Drain

When Athens experiences a downpour, the still functioning Great Drain collects runoff from the Acropolis, Areopagos and Agora, and sends it to the now mostly dry Eridanos river.

Agora Site Plan

Monument of the Eponymous Heroes

Citizens were divided into 10 tribes (phylae), each represented by a different Attican hero. This monument, dated 350 BC, had bronze statues of each representative tribal hero: Antiochos, Ajax, Leos, Hippothoon, Erechtheus, Aegeus, Cecrops, Akamas, Pandion and Oeneus.

Altar of Zeus Agoraios

This lavish temple to the ruler of the gods was originally built elsewhere in Athens (possibly the Pnyx) in the 4th century BC. In the first century AD, it was dismantled, brought to the Agora and reconstructed.

Site of Pilgrimage

You may well see people standing on the Areopagos, the rock above the Agora, praying or singing hymns. Pilgrims from around the world retracing the steps of Paul converge here, the site named in the Bible (Acts 17:22–34) where the saint gave his famous "Men of Athens ..." speech. The address spoke of the wrongs of ancient Greek religions, and here Paul converted the first Athenians to Christianity.

Middle Stoa

The large Middle Stoa took up the major part of the central marketplace, its two aisles lined with Doric columns.

Nymphaion

The ruins of the Nymphaion, an elaborate 2nd century fountain-house, are still visible, despite the building of a Byzantine church over it in the 11th century (above left).

Stoa of Attalos

King Attalos II of Pergamon (159–138 BC) built this impressive two-storey structure (right). It was reconstructed in 1956 by the American School of Archaeology. Today the Stoa is a world-class museum displaying finds from the Agora. (See pp14–15.)

 See following pages for the Agora Museum

Left **Ostrakon condemning Hippocrates to exile** Right **Stoa of Attalos**

Agora Museum (Stoa of Attalos)

1 Aryballos
This small Archaic oil-flask sculpted in the form of a kneeling boy represents an athlete binding a ribbon, a symbol of victory, around his head. It dates to around 530 BC.

2 Klepsydra
Dating to the 5th century BC, this is a unique example of the terracotta water clocks used for timing speeches in the public law courts. When a speaker began, the stopper was pulled out of the jug. It would take exactly six minutes for the water to run out, at which point the speaker had to stop, even if he was in mid-sentence.

Aryballos, Archaic oil-flask

3 Ostraka
These inscribed pottery fragments played a crucial role in the incipient democracy. Called *ostraka*, they were used as ballots in the process of ostracism. When there was fear of a tyranny, citizens voted to exile politicians considered dangerous to democracy. Those displayed show the names of several prominent politicians exiled in this way, including Themistokles, one of Athens' most important leaders.

4 Bronze Shield
This huge Spartan shield was a trophy taken by the Athenians after their victory over the Spartans in the battle of Sphacteria, in 425 BC. It is a vast object, and it's incredible to imagine a soldier carrying something so heavy and cumbersome into the melee of battle. On the front of the shield, one of the Athenian victors has inscribed, "Athens defeated Sparta at Pylos".

5 Head of Nike
This small, delicate head of Athena Nike *(right)*, dated to around 425 BC, was once covered with sheets of silver and gold; eyes would have been inset.

6 Winged Nike
This sensuous, swirling, rippling statue of Athena once adorned the Agora's Stoa of Zeus Eleutherios. Her active stance and clinging, flowing *chiton* (a loose, full-length tunic) are typical of the way in which the goddess was depicted at that time. It dates to around 415 BC.

7 Athenian Law for Democracy
In 336 or 337 BC, the citizens of Athena passed a historic vote for a new system of democracy, giving every (male) citizen an equal vote. The law is inscribed here, and topped by an image of a personification of the Demos (people) of Athens being crowned by Democracy herself.

Apollo Patroos

This colossal but finely sculpted cult statue of Apollo graced a temple to the god in the Agora. A later copy shows that in this sculpture the god of music was playing the kithara, an early stringed instrument. Dating to around 330 BC, it is the work of the famous sculptor and painter Euphranor.

Marble Cleroterion

This allotment machine was used by the Parliament of Athens between the 3rd and 2nd century BC, in the period of the ten tribes of Attica, to select officials. The seemingly simple box performed complex operations with slots, weights, cranks and coloured balls. A sign below the display case explains the complexities of its operation.

Calyx Krater

Dating to 530 BC, this is the earliest known calyx krater – an elegant vessel used to mix water and wine at banquets – and the only vase of this shape attributed to Exekias, the greatest Attic vase painter. It shows several beautifully detailed scenes, including Herakles being introduced to the gods of Olympus and the Greek and Trojan heroes' fight over the body of Patroclus.

The Stoa of Attalos

The Stoa of Attalos originally served as a 2nd-century BC shopping mall. Both arcades were divided into shops, and the cool marble-pillared space was a popular place for wealthy Athenians to meet and gossip. Through decades of excavations, the Agora has become recognized as one of Greece's most important sites, yielding finds precious for their artistic quality and ability to tell important stories about political and cultural life in the first democracy. In the 1950s, the American School of Archaeology reconstructed the Stoa and converted the building into a museum to display finds from the site. Most of the museum's exhibits are closely connected with the development of democracy in Athens. Outside, in the marble passage, are displayed statues that once adorned the temples in the marketplace.

Head of Nike

The reconstructed Stoa of Attalos, now home of the Agora Museum

⁑10 National Archaeological Museum

More than just the best museum in Greece, this is one of the most important and exciting museums in the world. It is packed with famous, influential and beautiful works from the great Bronze Age cultures described by Homer to the Golden Age of Classical Athens and beyond. The temporary closure of part of the museum since 1999 has afforded the chance to improve the display of the priceless finds amassed here.

The museum's imposing Neo-Classical façade

🔵 There's so much to see here that it makes sense to go twice – and to invest in one of the short informational guide books available at the museum.

🔵 There is an atrium café inside the museum and a larger café out front.

• 44 Patision
(28 Oktovriou)
• Map C1
• Metro: Victoria
• 210 821 7717
• www.culture.gr
• Apr–Oct: 8am–7pm
Tue–Sun, 1pm–7pm
Mon; Nov–Mar:
8:30am–3pm Tue–Sun,
1pm–7pm Mon
• Adm €7

Top 10 Exhibits

1. Cycladic Collection
2. Thira Frescoes
3. Mycenaean Collection
4. Hellenistic Statuary
5. Bronze Collection
6. Classical Statuary
7. Grave Stelae
8. Archaic Koroi
9. Vase Collection
10. Egyptian Wing

1 Cycladic Collection, 3,200–2,200 BC

The Cycladic Museum *(see pp18–19)* has the largest collection from this civilization, but here you'll find some of the most unusual pieces, such as this harp-player *(above)*, showing, unusually, a three-dimensional figure in action.

2 Thira Frescoes

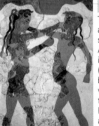

The highly advanced settlement of Akrotiri, on the island of Thira (Santorini), was buried under a volcanic eruption in the 16th century BC. Beautiful frescoes, such as these boxer boys *(left)*, were perfectly preserved under the ash.

3 Mycenaean Collection, 16th–11th Centuries BC

The Mycenaeans were famed both for their prowess as warriors and their hoards of gold. Parts of those shining hoards are displayed here, including this legendary death mask *(centre)* and priceless golden swords.

4 Hellenistic Statuary

Here the stiff, solid monuments of the Archaic period give way to sculptures that are full of vigorous movement and sensuality. This is especially so in the 100 BC group of Aphrodite, Pan and Eros, the statue of a wounded Gaul and this youth of Antikythira *(right)*.

5 Bronze Collection

Many of the greatest Archaic and Classical works were bronze, but few remain – most were melted down for weapons during invasions. This, the richest collection of the survivors, includes a majestic 460 BC sculpture of Poseidon or Zeus and this 140 BC sculpture of a galloping horse *(right)*.

6 Classical Statuary

Collected here are original marble sculptures from temples all around Greece. Highlights are those that adorned the Asklepion at Epidauros, and works like the 100 BC Diadoumenos and a marble copy of a 5th-century bronze by the great sculptor Polykleitos.

7 Grave Stelae

Classical marble grave sculptures *(below)* were so large and opulent that they were actually banned in 317 BC. The scenes in these beautiful carvings typically show the deceased on the right, the bereaved on the left.

8 Archaic Koroi, 7th Century BC–480 BC

Koroi (statues of youths and maidens used at temples and graves) were the first monumental works in Greek art. The earliest are stiff and stylized, but through the centuries the artists learnt to depict the body more naturalistically.

Earthquake

In September 1999, the strongest earthquake in a century rocked Athens, sending buildings tumbling and, in the National Archaeological Museum, shattering fragile pots and frescoes. About half the museum was subsequently closed to the public, but reopened with most of the objects restored in 2004.

Mycenaean death mask

10 Egyptian Wing

This is a recent addition to the museum, and is fascinating to view in conjunction with the earliest Greek Archaic art, which borrowed heavily from Egyptian statuary before developing into its very own style. Look out for the 715 BC bronze statue of the princess-priestess Takusit.

9 Vase Collection

These intricately painted vases show the development of pottery in Greece from Neolithic examples *(above)* to the 4th century BC. They were largely found in cemeteries and religious sanctuaries.

TOP 10 Museum of Cycladic Art

A delightful setting in which to ponder elegant, semi-abstract Cycladic figurines – remnants of a culture that flourished in the Cyclades from 3200–2000 BC. The beautiful marble carvings are unlike anything found in contemporary civilizations. Most are female forms – possibly cult objects of a goddess religion – and their elemental shapes have inspired many 20th-century artists.

Hunter-warrior and queen

Entrance to the New Wing

Top 10 Exhibits

1 "Modigliani" Figure
2 Dove Vessel
3 Hunter-warrior and queen
4 Male Figure
5 Cup-Bearer
6 Monumental Figure
7 Symposium Kylix
8 Dionysus Vase
9 New Wing
10 Gift Shop

🔎 All the featured exhibits are in the main building of the Cycladic wing. The new wing shows temporary exhibitions.

School and tour groups crowd the museum most mornings. If you want peace and quiet, leave your visit until after 1pm.

🍴 The museum's atrium café makes a great spot for a light lunch.

- Neofytou Douka 4 and Vasilissis Sofias
- Map P3
- 210 722 8321
- www.cycladic.gr
- Metro: Evangelismos
- 10am–4pm Mon–Fri, 10am–3pm Sat
- Adm: €5; students €2.50

"Modigliani" Figure 1

So-called because the lines of this figure *(right)* show up clearly in the work of 20th-century painter Amedeo Modigliani. The slender, simple shape, crossed arms and smooth face are all classic Cycladic traits. Non-standing feet indicate that such figures would probably have been lying down.

2 Dove Vessel

Carved entirely from one block of marble, this is the most remarkable of a series of "frying-pan" vessels found in tombs *(above)*. Archaeologists believe birds held an important symbolism for the Cycladic culture, as they appear in many other carvings as well – but as to the nature of that significance, the mystery remains.

3 Hunter-warrior and queen

The male and female figures *(top)*, with elongated arms and almond-shaped eyes and mouths, are the most naturalistic of the later Cycladic figures. Experts believe that the baldric and dagger carved around the male figure indicates that he was a hunter-warrior.

Male Figure 4

The only male figure of its size found so far in the prototypical Cycladic style *(right)*. Attributed to the Goulandris Master, who created the finest female figures, it has the same shape and placement of the arms but distinctly different genitals. The separated legs indicate a standing pose, rather than the typically prone pose of the female figures.

Cup-Bearer 5
Figures like this seated drinker, arm raised jovially, are extremely rare in Cycladic sculpture. The few that do exist show that, in addition to the prone goddess figures found in burials, the culture also produced active images of everyday life.

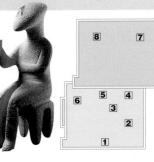

Monumental Figure 6
One of the largest Cycladic figures ever found, its size beautifully showcases the clear outlines, symmetry and style of the gifted artist. It also begins to suggest the Archaic style, which appeared centuries later. Its scale suggests that it was more likely used in a cult shrine than in a grave.

Dionysus Vase 8
This beautifully preserved 6th-century BC vase *(right)* shows god of wine and revelry Dionysus on one side (flanked by nude, dancing satyrs) and, on the other side, Athena and Hermes conversing.

New Wing 9
In 1991, the museum took over the adjoining Stathatos Mansion, a gorgeous gilded Neo-Classical confection designed by Bavarian architect Ernst Ziller *(see p96)*. Here, among lusciously restored chandeliers, velvet drapes and original antique furniture, the museum holds temporary exhibitions, receptions and occasional lectures.

Gift Shop 10
A destination in its own right for serious shoppers. You can see how modern and timeless the Cycladic figures are in these reinterpretations on silver jewellery and ceramics. There's also a wide selection of coffee-table and scholarly art books.

Key to Floors 1 & 2
█ First Floor
█ Second Floor

Symposium Kylix 7
An exceptional piece of 5th-century BC pottery that shows reclining youths in a symposium, where they gathered to lounge, drink wine and talk of philosophy (and, occasionally, coarser matters). The scene shows a pause in the high-minded discourse for the youths to play a game involving flipping their wine cups into the centre.

The Goulandris Dynasty

The museum's founders, the Goulandris family, are arguably Greece's greatest shipping dynasty (they had a long-standing rivalry with Onassis). They are also known for their legacy of arts: in addition to the Museum of Cycladic Art, the family have founded two museums on the island of Andros and are planning a new Museum of Modern Art in Athens.

TOP 10 Roman Forum & Tower of the Winds

In the first century AD, the Romans moved Athens' marketplace here from the old Agora. Smaller than the original, the marble-pillared courtyard was a grander place to set up shop, and this became the commercial and administrative centre until the 19th century. Its greatest attraction was the unique and brilliantly designed Tower of the Winds.

Euros, the southeast wind, Tower of the Winds

Propylon gateway

🌙 During the harvest moon in late August (considered to be the biggest, brightest moon of the year), there is a free moonlit classical concert here.

🍴 Most restaurants around the Roman Agora are touristy and overpriced. Head for nearby O Platanos, on Diogenous, which offers simple, tasty and reasonably priced taverna fare (see p75).

- Aiolou and Diogenous, Monastiraki
- Map J4–K4
- 210 324 5220
- www.culture.gr
- Apr–Oct: 8am–7:15pm daily; Nov–Mar: 8am–3pm daily
- Adm €2 (students half price) or included in €12 Acropolis ticket

Top 10 Sights

1. Tower of the Winds
2. Agoranomeion (Office of the Market Officials)
3. Vespasianae (68-seat Public Latrine)
4. Byzantine Grave Markers
5. East Propylon
6. Fetiye Mosque
7. Courtyard
8. Fountain
9. Gate of Athena Archegetis
10. Inscription of Julius Caesar and Augustus

Tower of the Winds
The octagonal tower, built by Syrian astronomer Andronikos Kyrrhestas in 50 BC, has personifications of the winds on each side. Inside, a water clock was operated by a stream from the Acropolis.

Partial restoration of the columns

Vespasianae (68-seat Public Latrine)
The pleasantly situated marble facility was housed in a rectangular building with a courtyard in the middle, and latrines lining all four sides. Proximity wasn't a problem – latrines were social gathering places.

Byzantine Grave Markers
In Byzantine times, when the Tower of the Winds was used as a church, the area around it was a cemetery. Graves were marked with cylindrical engraved markers, some quite beautiful. These were later gathered in one place, along with others from around Athens.

Agoranomeion
This two-roomed building was believed, until recently, to be the office of market officials. Current theories say it may have been part of a cult to Claudius or Nero.

East Propylon

This is one of the two original entrances to the marketplace *(right)*. In a stoa next to it are sculptures of important Romans, probably officials or emperors, which shoppers would have seen while coming and going.

Fetiye Mosque

During the Ottoman occupation, the Forum remained an important centre. In 1456, the Turks built this "Mosque of the Conqueror" *(below)* directly over the ruins of an early Christian church.

Courtyard

This was the centre of activity. The courtyard was surrounded by shops and workshops selling food, cloth, ceramics, jewellery and wares from abroad. The Emperor Hadrian had the courtyard paved in the second century AD.

Gate of Athena Archegetis

The monumental four-columned western entrance to the forum is built of beautiful Pentelic marble. It was built in 11 BC by Julius Caesar and Augustus, and dedicated by the people of Athens to the goddess Athena.

Fountain

This splashing marble fountain, whose waters, like those of the water clock, may also have been sourced from the Acropolis, once provided cool relief to market-goers. But stay away from the brackish water that occasionally fills it today.

Inscription of Julius Caesar and Augustus

The inscription denoting that the Gate of Athena Archegetis was built by Caesar and Augustus is so faded that it can now only be seen at noon precisely. Stand outside the forum, and look directly at the top of the entrance.

A Miscellany of Finds

Ever since the 1940s, archaeologists have used the forum as a repository for small, unclassifiable finds from all over Attica. Thus the site is studded with out-of-place but fascinating extras, like the wall of mismatched capital pieces near the Vespasianae (latrine), or the garlanded sarcophagus, about which little is known, by the fountain.

TOP 10 Benaki Museum

This vast museum gives a panoramic view of Greek history from the Stone Age (7000 BC) to the 20th century, by way of Classical Greece and the eras of the Byzantine and Ottoman empires. Over 20,000 objects are laid out in chronological order in 36 rooms, showing the evolution of Greek painting, sculpture and handicrafts.

The rooftop café

🕐 Bear in mind that there is free admission and late night opening on Thursdays.

📝 It is almost impossible to see the entire Benaki collection in one go: explore one section in the morning, stop for lunch in the rooftop café, then see the rest in the afternoon.

- Koumpari 1, Kolonaki
- Map N3
- 210 367 1000
- www.benaki.gr
- Metro: Syntagma
- 9am–5pm Mon, Wed, Fri & Sat; 9am–midnight Thu; 9am–3pm Sun;
- Closed Tue
- Adm €6; free Thu

Top 10 Exhibits

1. The Building
2. Evia Treasure
3. Thebes Treasure
4. Thessaly Treasure
5. Paintings by El Greco
6. Mid-18th-Century Reception Room
7. A Second Room from Kozani
8. Greek Independence Memorabilia
9. Café
10. Shop

The Building

A magnificent white Neo-Classical mansion of 1867. It was bought by Emmanuel Benakis in 1910, passed to his children, then was presented to the state in 1931 when it opened as a museum.

Evia Treasure

Around 3000 BC, the introduction of metallurgy marked the transition from the Stone Age to the Bronze Age. Outstanding examples from this period are these three cups, two gold (one of which is shown above) and one silver, hammered into simple forms with minimal decoration. They date from 3000–2800 BC.

Key

■	Ground Floor
■	First Floor
■	Second Floor
■	Third Floor

Thebes Treasure

During the late Bronze Age, ornamental jewellery was used to display personal wealth. This hoard of Mycenaean gold jewellery includes an engraved gold signet ring *(above)*, depicting a sacred marriage connected to the worship of a prehistoric goddess.

Entrance

Thessaly Treasure 4

This stunning display of Hellenistic and Roman gold jewellery from the 3rd–2nd centuries BC employs filigree and granulation (beads of gold soldered onto metal) to produce minutely crafted earrings, necklaces, bracelets and diadems. The decorative band above has a knot of Herakles at its centre.

Paintings by El Greco 5

Domenikos Theotokopoulos (1541–1614) became known as El Greco while living in Spain. Two early works here, completed while the artist was still in his native Crete, include *The Adoration of the Magi (right)*, influenced by the Venetian School.

Mid-18th-Century Reception Room 6

The richly painted and gilded wooden ceiling and panelled walls of this room *(left)* – a reconstruction from a Macedonian mansion – recall a time when these crafts flourished in the region, as local merchants prospered under Ottoman rule.

A Second Room from Kozani 7

Another reconstruction from Macedonia, this mid-18th-century reception room features a minutely carved wooden ceiling, ornate built-in wooden cupboards and a low seating area, complete with Persian rugs and cushions, and a wrought-iron coffee table.

Greek Independence Memorabilia 8

Finely decorated swords, sabres and rifles, a painting of a long-haired moustachioed freedom fighter from 1821 *(right)* and a portable writing desk belonging to Lord Bryon are among the displays.

Café 9

Cultural overload? Take a break on the rooftop terrace café overlooking the trees and lawns of the National Gardens.

Shop 10

Here, exhibits such as ceramic bowls and tiles, jewellery and Byzantine icons have been carefully reproduced, using original craft techniques where possible.

Who Was Benakis?

Antonis Benakis (1873–1954) was born in Egypt to an immensely wealthy merchant, Emmanuel Benakis, who later became Mayor of Athens. Antonis began collecting Islamic art while in Alexandria and went on to collect Byzantine art and Greek folk art once in Athens. He donated the entire collection to the Greek state in 1931. His sister, Penelope Delta (1874–1941), was a much-loved author of children's books.

Kerameikos

The outer walls of ancient Athens run through Kerameikos, once the edge of the Classical city. Warriors and priestesses returned to Athens via two separate roads through here (one to a brothel, the other to a temple). Statesmen and heroes were buried beneath showy tombs lining the roads. And it was also the scene of far shadier activities: the haunt of prostitutes, money-lenders and wine-sellers.

Stele of Demetria and Pamphile

Statesmen's tombs

🕐 The green site and surrounding industrial buildings are at their most eerily lovely in the early evening, tinged pink by the setting sun.

🍴 Several reasonably priced tavernas line the nearby streets of Adrianou and Apostolou Pavlou. Head to either for a traditional outdoor lunch.

- Ermou 148, Thissio
- 210 331 0137; 210 331 4324
- Map A3–4
- Metro: Kerameikos
- Apr–Oct: 8am–7pm daily; Nov–Mar: 8am–3pm daily
- Adm €2
- Oberlander Museum
- Apr–Oct: 8am–7pm daily; Nov–Mar: 8am–3pm daily

Top 10 Sights

1. City Walls
2. Dipylon
3. Pompeiion
4. Sacred Gate
5. Warriors' Tombs
6. Sanctuary of the Tritopatores
7. Tomb of Dexileos
8. Marble Bull, Tomb of Dionysios of Kollytos
9. Stele of Hegeso
10. Oberlander Museum

City Walls
The walls, which surrounded the entire city, were built by Athenian ruler Themistockles in 478 BC. Made in haste, the walls incorporated materials from all over the city, including marble from tombs, temples and houses.

Dipylon
The grand entrance to Athens was the largest gate in ancient Greece. The main roads from Thebes, Corinth and the Peloponnese led to this gate, and many ceremonial events were held here to mark arrivals and departures.

Pompeiion
The Pompeiion *(right)* was used to prepare for festive and religious processions, especially the annual Panathenaic procession, in which a new garment was brought to the statue of Athena in the Parthenon.

Sacred Way

Sacred Gate
Through this well-preserved gate passed the Sacred Way, reserved for pilgrims and priestesses during the procession to Eleusis *(see p111)*. A great marble sphinx was built into the gate.

Previous pages **Temple of Olympian Zeus**

Warriors' Tombs

The high, round burial mounds (tumuli) lining the holy road date from the 7th century BC and were probably first built to honour great warriors. Most have marble coffins and offerings at their centres, with the mounds built up around them.

Site Plan

Sanctuary of the Tritopatores

It is uncertain who exactly the Tritopatores were, but they may have been representatives of the souls of the dead, and been worshipped in an ancestor cult.

Tomb of Dexileos

This marble-relief carved tomb *(above)* is of a young horseman who died in 394 BC. The dead of ancient Greece were often depicted along with their living family, saying a final goodbye.

Marble Bull

The bull of the tomb of Dionysios of Kollytos is perhaps the most recognizable monument here. Its inscriptions tell us that Dionysios was praised for his goodness, and died unmarried, mourned by his mother and sisters.

The Old Potters' District

The name Kerameikos comes from Keramos, the patron god of ceramics. According to Pausanias *(see p37)* and other early writers, the name recalls an age-old group of potters' workshops on the grassy banks of the river Eridanos, which cuts through the site. The museum contains fine examples of Greek urns and other pottery found at the site.

Stele of Hegeso

This lovely grave pediment is one of the finest s of 5th-century BC rt. Hegeso, the dead , is seated, taking from a box. The in the National ical Museum.

Oberlander Museum

This small museum is packed with fascinating finds, including originals of many tombs replaced by casts. Don't miss pottery shards of erotic scenes from a brothel.

sights and pleasures in areas neighbouring   meikos see pp78–85

Byzantine Museum

From the fall of Rome in 476 to the fall of Constantinople in 1453, the Byzantine Empire dominated the Mediterranean region. The mysterious and wealthy Orthodox Church was the most important political and artistic influence in Byzantium, leaving behind a vast legacy. This world-renowned collection embraces 15,000 objects taken from that fascinating period.

Museum façade and courtyard

🎵 In summer, there are often concerts in the courtyard. Year-round, there are frequent guided tours free of charge, but times and English-language availability vary. Call ahead to find out what's on and when.

🍴 The museum plans to open a café on the premises by summer 2008. Until it does, head to one of the cafés or restaurants on Plateia Kolonaki.

- Vasilissis Sofias 22
- Map P3
- 210 723 2178
- www.culture.gr
- Metro: Evangelismos
- 8am–3pm Tue–Sun
- Adm €4

Top 10 Exhibits

1. Orpheus Playing a Lyre
2. Shepherd Carrying a Lamb
3. Icon of Archangel Michael
4. Manuscript Collection
5. Mosaic Icon of the Virgin (The Episkepsis) Treasury of Mytilene
6. Precious Ecclesiastical Artifacts
7. Wall Painting from the Church of Episkopi
8. Double-Sided Icon of St George
9. Treasury of Mytilene
10. Temporary Exhibitions

Orpheus Playing a Lyre

Orpheus *(above)* is surrounded by animals, creating an allegory of Christ and his followers. This transmutation of ancient pagan myths into the new religion of Christianity was an essential element of Byzantine art.

Shepherd Carrying a Lamb

This 4th-century marble sculpture is also a Christian allegory with pagan roots. Though the shepherd is meant to be Christ, the image is taken directly from an Archaic sculpture found on the Acropolis of a man bringing a calf to be sacrificially slaughtered to the goddess Athena *(see image on p10).*

Key

■ Upper Floor
□ Lower Floor

Icon of Archangel Michael

Set in a glowing field of gold, this 14th-century *(left)* from Constantino depicts the Archange sceptre and an orb, of the terrestrial w

4 Manuscript Collection

The highlight of this collection is a 14th-century imperial document *(below)* issued by Emperor Andronicus

II. The top of the scroll bears a miniature showing the emperor himself handing a document to Christ, while at the bottom, the emperor's signature appears in red ink.

5 Mosaic icon of the Virgin (The Episkepsis)

This 13th Century mosaic *(right)* shows the Virgin and Child, with a gold background symbolising divine light. Mosaic icons are very rare: Only about 40 are known to exist, all of which, like this one, originate from Constantinople.

6 Precious Ecclesiastical Artifacts

This case contains a late 14th-century wooden cross covered with silver and embellished with small steatite icons, a 10th-century copper chalice, and a 14th-century silk stole decorated with holy figures embroidered in metalic and silk thread.

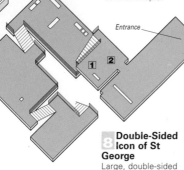

Entrance

7 Wall Painting from the Church of Episkopi

Executed between the 10th and 13th-centuries, these paintings depict biblical scenes in warm, muted hues. They are displayed in the positions as they would have been in the church, which was based on a 'cross in square' plan with a dome and Narthex.

8 Double-Sided Icon of St George

Large, double-sided icons were extremely rare in Byzantium. This 13th-century example is especially unusual as it is carved in three dimensions and depicts the full body.

9 Treasury of Mytilene

A collection of 6th-century silver vessels, gold jewellery and coins, discovered in a sunken ship off the island of Mytilene (Lesvos). Scholars believe the valuables were brought to the island to be hidden, and were never recovered by their owners.

10 Temporary Exhibitions

Take the time to look beyond the permanent collection to the Temporary Exhibitions Wing. The Orthodox Church works in co-operation with institutions around the world to show and exhibit rarely seen Byzantine artifacts, such as items from the monastery of St Catherine, Mount Sinai.

Aristotle's Lyceum

Building plans for the neighbouring site were shelved when excavators discovered ancient ruins identified as the Lyceum of Aristotle (the school the philosopher founded to compete with Plato's Academy). The site has been taken over by the Byzantine Museum, with plans to open it to the public by 2007.

Filopappos Hill

The pine-covered slopes of Filopappos Hill offer a pleasantly shaded maze of paths leading through monuments marking centuries of history. Known as "the hill of muses" in antiquity, countless poets have drawn inspiration here. On the first day of Lent, the hill is swarmed with hundreds of Athenians, who traditionally gather here to fly kites.

Church of Agios Dimitrios Loumbardiaris

View from Filopappos Hill

🕐 Though perfectly safe during the day, the paths of Filopappos Hill are best avoided after dark.

🍴 There is a pleasant café called the Loumbardiaris in the trees just behind the Church of Agios Dimitrios Loumbardiaris.

- Enter from Dionysiou Areopagitou (Map C5)
- Map B6
- www.culture.gr
- Metro: Akropoli
- Free
- Dora Stratou Dance Theatre: performances late May–late Sep: 9:30pm Tue–Sat, 8:15pm Sun. Tickets from theatre, or call 210 324 4395

Top 10 Sights

1. Hilltop View
2. Filopappos Monument
3. Socrates' Prison
4. Church of Agios Dimitrios Loumbardiaris
5. The Pnyx
6. The Deme of Koile
7. Church of Agia Marina
8. Old National Observatory
9. Hill of the Nymphs
10. Dora Stratou Dance Theatre

Hilltop View
You may not feel you deserve such a jaw-dropping view after such an easy, shaded walk. But the hilltop directly overlooks the Acropolis and all of southern Athens stretching to the sea. This was once a favourite vantage-point for generals – and it's equally appealing to photographers today.

Filopappos Monument
Roman senator Gaius Julius Antiochus Filopappos was a lover of Classical Greek culture. He took his retirement in Athens and died here in about AD 114. The Greeks built this marble tomb and monument to the senator, showing him as an Athenian citizen, surrounded by his royal Roman family. Its partially destroyed form *(left)* looks across to the Acropolis.

Filopappos Hill

Socrates' Prison
This is believed to be the cave where Socrates *(see p36)* was imprisoned, having been condemned to death. His disciples sat with him as he drank the hemlock that dispatched him.

Church of Agios Dimitrios Loumbardiaris
In 1648, an Ottoman commander planned to bombard this charming Byzantine church. But lightning struck his cannon, giving the church the name of "St Dimitri the Bomber".

The Pnyx

If Athens is the cradle of democracy, this spot is its exact birthplace. After Athens became a democracy in 508 BC, the first ever democratic congress met here weekly, and the greatest orators held forth. The limestone theatre, cut into the hill *(right)*, accommodated over 10,000.

The Deme of Koile

This ancient road leads from the Acropolis to Piraeus, passing between Filopappos Hill and the Pnyx to follow the course of the Long Walls (5th century BC). It was a two-lane road, 8–12 m (26–40 ft) wide, with anti-slip grooves. A 500-m (1600-ft) stretch has been excavated.

Church of Agia Marina

Agia Marina is associated with childbirth and sick children, and so pregnant women come here and slip down a carved slide to ensure a safe delivery. In the past, mothers brought sick children here to spend the night. A colourful festival honours Marina each July.

Old National Observatory

Greece's oldest research centre is housed in a beautiful Neo-Classical building *(left)*. The centre monitors astronomy, weather, and especially the earthquakes that occasionally rattle Athens.

Hill of the Nymphs

ncient times, Greeks ved Filopappos was ted by the muses of sic and poetry. And aller hill was the place of nymphs le spirits of and springs.

Dora Stratou Dance Theatre

Dora Stratou's troupe travels the land, learning and keeping alive hundreds of regional dances. Here, they present the intricate moves that have been part of Greek culture for centuries.

The 1687 Siege

During an attempt to seize the Ottoman-occupied Acropolis, the Venetians garrisoned themselves on Filopappos Hill, the perfect strategic location to shell their target. Too perfect, unfortunately – a shell hit the Parthenon, where the Turks stored their gunpowder, and the ensuing explosion severely damaged the Acropolis's prized temple and sculptures.

⬛10 Temple of Olympian Zeus

The majestic temple to the ruler of the pantheon was the largest on mainland Greece. Inside stood two colossal gold and ivory statues: one of the god, and one of the Roman Emperor Hadrian. Though the temple's construction began in 515 BC, political turmoil delayed its completion nearly 700 years. To thank Hadrian for finishing it, in AD 131 the Athenians built a two-storey arch next to the temple, whose inscription announces Hadrian's claim on the city.

Remaining columns of the Temple of Olympian Zeus

🕑 To get the best light for photographs of the column capitals, come between 3 and 4pm.

🍴 For a bite to eat, head across the street to Zappeion Gardens to either elegant Aigli café and restaurant or one of the handful of other cafés spread through the park.

• Vas. Olgas at Amalias
• Map L5
• 210 922 6330
• www.culture.gr
• Summer: 8:30am–7pm daily; winter: 8:30am–3pm daily
• Adm €2, or included with Acropolis ticket

Top 10 Sights

1. Temple of Olympian Zeus
2. Hadrian's Arch
3. Ruins of Houses
4. Themistoklean Gates
5. Roman Baths
6. Valerian Wall
7. Temple of Apollo Delphinios and Artemis Delphinia
8. Law Court at the Delphinion
9. Temple of Kronos and Rhea
10. Temple of Zeus Panhellenios

Temple of Olympian Zeus ⬛1
Zeus had long been worshipped on this site, and there was at least one other temple to him before this one. Sixteen magnificent columns survive from the original 104.

Hadrian's Arch ⬛2
Emperor Hadrian had the west side of this arch *(below)* inscribed "This is Athens, the ancient city of Theseus", and the east side "This is the city of Hadrian and not of Theseus", distinguishing the cities of ancient legend and modern reality.

Ruins of Houses ⬛3
Ancient pipes, foundations, and domestic objects show that people lived and built houses here between the 5th century BC and 2nd century AD – the whole time it took to build the temple.

Themistoklean Gates ⬛4
Around the site are remains of the wall b by political leader Themistokles in 47° to defend Athens continuing onsla· the Persians.

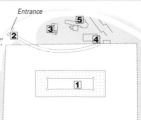
Entrance

Roman Baths
5 Among the many ruins of "Hadrianopolis", the first structures of Hadrian's new city, are these complex-looking foundations *(left)*, actually the best-preserved Roman bath house in Athens. It once had a coloured mosaic floor.

Valerian Wall
6 The Roman emperor Valerian commissioned this wall *(below)* in the third century AD. Many of the temples it surrounded were demolished to provide marble for the wall. Having been temporarily closed to the public, it reopened in 2004.

Temple of Apollo Delphinios and Artemis Delphinia
7 The temple was built to the god-and-goddess siblings Apollo and Artemis, celebrating them in the form of dolphins.

Temple of Kronos and Rhea
9 This temple to Zeus's parents was built in the _th century BC; now only _ foundations remain. _a saved Zeus from _os, and Zeus then _dominion of the uni_ _as ruler of the gods.

Law Court at the Delphinion
8 Now mostly in ruins, this law court, from 500 BC, is thought to be on the site of the palace of mythical king Aegeus, the father of Theseus *(see p39)*.

Temple of Zeus Panhellenios
10 Hadrian promoted the cult of Zeus Panhellenios ("ruler of all the Greeks") and associated himself with the god. Offers to god and emperor were made in this temple, later demolished for the Valerian wall.

Why Did it Take so Long to Build?
The tyrant Peisistratos started the temple in 515 BC to occupy the rebellious Athenians. After his fall, the democratic Athenians refused to finish what they saw as a monument to a hated tyrant. In 174 BC, King Antiochus IV of Epiphanes took over the work, but it stopped with his death in 163 BC. When Hadrian came in AD 124, he finally saw the temple completed.

Left **Ancient Athens** Right **German soldiers at the Acropolis in World War II**

TOP 10 **Moments in History**

1 Birth of Athens
The Acropolis was first inhabited in Neolithic times (around 3000 BC), and began to take on the form of a city when it was fortified by the Mycenaeans (inhabitants of the southeastern Greek mainland) in about 1400 BC.

2 Golden Age
The 6th and 5th centuries BC saw the city-state develop into a colonial power. Under Perikles (495–429 BC) Athens enjoyed its greatest period of building, when the Parthenon, Erechtheion and Temple of Nike were erected. Cultural and intellectual life flourished until Sparta's defeat of Athens in the Peloponnesian War (431–404 BC).

3 Roman Athens
Roman rule began in 146 BC and lasted five centuries. Athenians initially maintained good relations with their rulers, but in 86 BC a potential move towards Athenian independence was brutally crushed by the Romans. Emperor Hadrian (AD 76–138) remained a great admirer of Greek culture, however, and together with Greek scholar Herodes Atticus he set up various building schemes, including the great theatre (see p9).

4 Byzantine Period
When Roman territory was divided between East and West in AD 395, Greece fell within the east, and subsequently became part of the Byzantine Empire.

The pagan philosophical schools were closed and many temples were rebuilt as churches.

5 Ottomans Take Athens
The Ottoman Turks took Athens in 1458, and the city became a provincial backwater. After bombarding the Parthenon, the Venetians held the city briefly in 1687. Then, during the 18th century, English and French artists and writers visited Athens as part of the Grand Tour, signalling its reawakening but also walking off with many ancient artworks.

6 War of Independence
In 1821 Greeks rose up against Ottoman domination, initially alone and then, as of 1827, with the aid of Britain, France and Russia. Although the war ended in 1829, the Ottomans held the Acropolis until 1834, when the new king, Otto I, entered the city. Athens became capital of the new Greek state and was rebuilt, largely in Neo-Classical style.

7 World War II
Mussolini declared war on Greece in October 1940, and the German army entered Athens in April 1941, raising the swastika over the Acropolis. The Third Reich used the Hotel Grande Bretagne (p140) as wartime headquarters.

8 Post World War II
At the close of WWII, with its political future uncertain, Greece fell into civil war. The

Raising the flag of Greek Independence

began pouring economic and military aid into the country, but on the proviso that the Communist Left would not gain power. In the 1950s and '60s, Athens saw rapid industrialization, mass migration from rural areas and the growth of sprawling suburbs.

Military Dictatorship
In April 1967, a coup d'etat led by Georgios Papadopoulos signalled the beginning of a seven-year military junta. Student protests on 17 November 1973 were violently put down by the military, who stormed Athens' Polytechnic and killed many. But the regime fell in 1974, following a failed attempt to take Cyprus.

Modern-Day Athens
Greece joined the EEC (now the EU) in 1981, and in the same year Andreas Papandreou became the country's first Socialist prime minister. In 1985, Athens was first European City of Culture. ...ing the highly successful ...Olympics means that the ...w has improved transport, ...nd cultural facilities.

Top 10 Athenians

1 Athena
In Ancient Greek mythology, Athena (see also pp38–9) became the patron of Athens.

2 Theseus
Legendary Athenian king who represented the qualities of youth, beauty, intelligence, good fortune and heroism.

3 Draco
In the 7th century BC, Draco instituted the first Code of Law: even trivial crimes incurred the death penalty, hence the term draconian.

4 Solon
Draco's laws were made less severe by Solon (c.638–559 BC); he also extended citizenship to the lower classes.

5 Cleisthenes
Statesman of around 570–507 BC, who abolished the rule of the aristocracy, replacing it with a democratic Assembly.

6 Themistokles
This general (c.527–460 BC) championed the navy as a force to expand the empire.

7 Perikles
Perikles (c.495–429 BC) got poorer citizens to attend the Assembly, beautified Athens and extended the empire.

8 Aspasia
In the 5th century BC, courtesan Aspasia gained acceptance in Athens' male-dominated intellectual and political circles.

9 Demosthenes
The greatest Greek orator (384–322 BC) overcame a speech impediment by talking with pebbles in his mouth.

10 Melina Mercouri
Much-loved actress (1925–94) who opposed the 1967–74 junta, became Minister of Culture and initiated the European City of Culture scheme.

or Athens' great philosophers and writers see pp36–7

Left **Plato's Banquet** Centre **Euripides** Right **Aristotle**

Philosophers and Writers

Socrates

1 Homer c.700 BC
Next to nothing is known about the bard who compiled the tales of *The Iliad* and *The Odyssey*. These poems, which were kept alive by oral tradition, are arguably the greatest and most influential in history.

2 Aeschylus 535–456 BC
When the "Father of Tragedy" began writing, theatre was in its infancy. He brought a wealth of characters, powerful narratives, grandeur of language, and a sweeping vision of humans working out a plan of cosmic justice to works such as *Prometheus Unbound* and the *Oresteia*.

3 Sophocles 496–406 BC
Only seven of Sophocles' plays survive, but his reputation rests securely

on three: *Antigone*, *Oedipus at Colonus*, and *Oedipus Rex*. The last of these, the story of a king bound hopelessly by fate to murder his father and marry his mother, is the greatest masterpiece of Greek tragedy.

4 Euripides 484–407 BC
Euripides was the last of the great triumvirate of Greek tragedians. He wrote radical re-interpretations of the ancient myths in which humans bore their suffering without reference to the gods or fates. His most famous plays, *The Bacchae* and *Medea*, are about mothers murdering their children.

5 Socrates 470–399 BC
Though Socrates himself wrote nothing, his teachings, re-corded in the writings of historians and especially his pupil Plato, have earned him the title of the forerunner of Western philosophy. At the height of the Golden Age of Athens, the original market-place philosopher debated the great meanings in the Agora, and was eventually tried and put to death for corrupting the Athenian youth *(see p30)*.

Homer

6 Aristophanes 447–385 BC
The greatest comic play wright of Greece was a welcome breath of f air after the age of great tragedians. Aristophanes' rau

hilarious *Lysistrata*, in which the women of warring Sparta and Athens refuse to sleep with their husbands until they stop fighting, is one of the greatest anti-war messages of all time.

Plato 428–348 BC
If Socrates was the forerunner of Western philosophy, Plato was the foundation. His works, from his early dialogues reprising Socrates' teachings, to later masterworks such as the seminal *Republic*, comprised the backbone of every major intellectual movement to follow.

Aristotle 384–322 BC
After studying with Plato, Aristotle tutored Alexander the Great. He later set up the Lyceum, a competitor to Plato's Academy. His *Poetics* is still one of the most important works of literary criticism, and his *Nichomachean Ethics* among the greatest treatises on ethics.

Nikos Kazantzakis 1883–1957
Millions have been drawn to the strange, joyous, bittersweet spirit of modern Greece as depicted in Kazantzakis' most famous work, *Zorba the Greek*. Darker in mood is the *Last Temptation of Christ* and best of all is his audacious continuation of the fundamental Greek tale: *The Odyssey: A Modern Sequel*.

George Seferis 1900–71
Greece's first Nobel Laureate was born in Smyrna which was later claimed by Turkey, and his lyrical poetry is inspired by history and feelings of exile. His work also relates Greece's Classical past to its raw present, as in *Mythistorema*, a series of poems that draw from *The Odyssey*.

Top 10 Tomes

1 *The Iliad*, Homer
One small episode in the Trojan War, told in the greatest epic ever written.

2 *The Odyssey*, Homer
Odysseus's adventures with sirens, nymphs and Cyclops on his way home from Troy.

3 *The Oresteia*, Aeschylus
Brilliant trilogy about the the House of Atreus, the most dysfunctional family in ancient Greece.

4 *The Theban Tragedies*, Sophocles
Terrible events unfold when Oedipus kills his father and marries his mother. Read on a visit to Delphi and Thebes.

5 *Republic*, Plato
Still the blueprint for the best way to run a government.

6 *Constitution of Athens*, Aristotle
A work that marries the democratic political structure of Athens with the architectural structure of the Agora.

7 *History of the Peloponnesian War*, Thucydides
Month-by-month, blow-by-blow account of the conflict by an Athenian officer.

8 *The Histories*, Herodotus
Compelling reportage of the Greeks' fight for freedom against the Persians, as told by the "Father of History".

9 *The Guide to Greece*, Pausanias
Pausanias, the world's first travel writer, recorded observations from all over Greece in his 2nd-century journey.

10 *Zorba the Greek*, Nikos Kazantzakis
The quintessential modern Greek novel.

Left **Perseus killing Medusa** Centre **Athena** Right **Zeus and Hera**

🔟 Athenian Legends

1 The Birth of Athena
When Zeus impregnated his mistress Metis, he was told she would have a son who would dethrone him. As a preventative measure, he swallowed Metis whole, but the unborn child continued to grow in Zeus's head. After nine months, Hephaestus split open the god's head with an axe, and out sprung the girl goddess Athena, already in full armour.

2 The Naming of Athens
Athena and Poseidon, god of the sea, competed for patronage of the great city in Attica by offering their best gifts. Poseidon struck his trident into the rock of the Acropolis and out gushed salt water. But Athena offered the olive tree, and the Olympian gods awarded her the city.

3 The Birth of Erichtonius
Hephaestus tried to rape Athena, but only managed to spill his seed on her leg. Athena brushed it to the ground, where it grew into the baby Erichtonius ("earth-born"). Athena raised him to become a king, and he is considered the first ancestor of all Athenians.

4 The Rape of Philomela
Erichtonius's son Pandion had two daughters, Procne and Philomela. When Procne's husband Tereus raped Philomela and cut out her tongue, Procne took revenge by serving the flesh of their son to Tereus. The sisters then turned for help to the gods, who made Philomela into a swallow, Tereus into a hoopoe and Procne into a nightingale (which cries "Tereu").

5 The Trial of Orestes
Orestes, after murdering his mother, Klytemnestra (to avenge her murder of his father, Agammemnon), was pursued to Athens by the Furies (underworld goddesses of vengeance). Athena decreed that instead of being killed, Orestes should stand trial. He was acquitted, and the trial marked a turning point in Athens, from blood feuds to rule of law.

6 Athena and Arachne
As goddess of spinning and weaving, Athena decided to help a poor but talented weaver called Arachne. Arachne won great admiration but took all the praise without crediting the goddess, and so Athena challenged her protégé to a weaving contest. Arachne's work depicted the inappropriate

Theseus killing the Minotaur

love affairs of the gods; Athena, furious with indignation, turned Arachne into the first spider.

7 Theseus's Arrival in Athens

Theseus, son of Athens' King Aegeus, was secretly raised far from court. At 16, armed with a sword left by his father, Theseus left for Athens, en route slaying dozens of monsters terrorizing Attica. He became Athens' greatest king and hero.

8 Theseus Kills the Minotaur

After a dispute between Aegeus and his brother Minos, King of Crete, Minos demanded Athens send regular tributes of 14 youths and maidens, who were sacrificed to the monstrous Minotaur. One year, Theseus asked to be sent and, with the help of Minos's daughter, Ariadne, he killed the Minotaur, saving hundreds of future Athenians.

9 The Death of Aegeus

Theseus had told his father that if his quest to kill the Minotaur was successful, he'd change his ship's sails from black to white on his return. But, after all the excitement, he forgot. When Aegeus, watching out for the ship from Sounio, saw the black sails, he was stricken with grief and plunged to his death in the sea (now called the Aegean).

10 Perseus Kills Medusa

Perseus was the son of Zeus and the maiden Danae. The tyrant Polydectes violently desired Danae, but Perseus promised him the snake-infested head of Medusa in exchange for his mother's safety. Perseus slew Medusa with Athena's help and, upon his return, turned Polydectes to stone; Athena then put Medusa's head on her shield.

Gods and Monsters

1 Zeus
The Pantheon's supreme god ruled the skies and fathered hundreds of heroes with his supernatural libido.

2 Poseidon
The god of the sea was Zeus's brother – and sometimes his greatest rival.

3 Athena
Zeus's daughter was a virgin warrior goddess of wisdom and philosophy. She was also goddess of weaving and patron of Athens.

4 Apollo
The handsome god of music and poetry presided over the Muses.

5 Artemis
Apollo's twin sister was goddess of the moon and the hunt, and remained a virgin.

6 Aphrodite
Voluptuous Aphrodite was Artemis's polar opposite – the temperamental goddess of love had dozens of affairs.

7 The Minotaur
Crete's Queen Pasiphae conceived this bull-headed, human-bodied monster with a bull sent by Poseidon.

8 The Cyclops
The most famous of these one-eyed giants is Polyphemus, the monster whom Odysseus blinded in *The Odyssey*.

9 The Sirens
The beautiful sirens with their bewitching songs nearly lured Odysseus's sailors to their deaths on a rocky shore.

10 Medusa
The gaze of this snake-headed gorgon turned men to stone. Perseus defeated her only with the help of Athena's gleaming shield, in which he could safely see his foe.

Left **Relief depicting a trireme** Right **Theatrical mask**

Greek Inventions

1 Olympic Games
The first recorded games were staged on the plains of Olympia in 776 BC. Dedicated to Zeus, they lasted one day and featured running and wrestling. In 472 BC – with the addition of boxing, the pancration (another form of hand-to-hand combat), horse racing and the pentathlon (sprinting, long-jump, javelin, discus and wrestling) – the event was extended to five days and held every four years.

2 Athenian Trireme
Masterpieces of ancient shipbuilding (c.700–500 BC), triremes were the key to Athens' naval strength. Approximately 40 m (130 ft) long and 5 m (15 ft) wide, they were noted for great speed – up to 12 knots per hour. The boats were powered by 170 oarsmen seated on three tiers. Only one tier rowed at a time, alternating short shifts so they did not exhaust themselves all at once. The vessels were also equipped with sails, which were lowered during battle.

Amphora depicting a race

3 Democracy
Demokratia ("power to the people") as a form of government was first introduced in Athens under Cleisthenes (570–507 BC).

All free, male, adult citizens of Athenian birth were entitled to attend the Assembly – which met on the Pnyx Hill – and thus participate in political decision-making. The Assembly gathered about 40 times a year, and 6,000 citizens needed to be present to make a vote valid.

4 Theatre
The earliest form of theatre can be traced back to an ancient Greek pagan ritual, which developed into an annual drama competition in the 6th century BC *(see p64)*. Plays were performed outside in daylight in purpose-built amphitheatres, and actors wore a range of masks to indicate different characters. The oldest plays emphasize values such as Greek patriotism, reverence to the gods, liberty and hospitality.

5 Pythagoras's Theorem
"The square of the hypotenuse of a right-angled triangle is equal to the sum of the squares of the other two sides." This theorem, discovered by the philosopher and mathematician Pythagoras (582–500 BC) was a major scientific breakthrough, which led to extraordinary advances in mathematics, geometry and astronomy.

6 Hippocratic Oath

Attributed to the founding father of medicine, the Greek physician Hippocrates (460–377 BC), this oath prohibits doctors from performing abortions, euthanasia or unnecessary surgery, and requires them to promise to abstain from sexual relations with any patient, and to keep any information divulged to them confidential. The oath was taken by doctors until 1948, when the World Medical Association (considering references to ancient Greek gods and goddesses somewhat obsolete) produced a modern restatement called the Declaration of Geneva.

Bust of Pythagoras

7 Catapult

Invented by Dionysius the Elder of Syracuse (430–367 BC), the catapult can hurl heavy objects or shoot arrows over large distances. Having seized power in Sicily, Dionysius set about driving out the Carthaginians, who ruled a large part of the island. Thanks in part to the catapult, he was successful, making Syracuse the strongest power in Greek Italy. The Romans later perfected his invention, adding wheels to catapults to make them mobile.

8 Archimedes' Screw

The Syracusan-born Greek mathematician Archimedes (287–212 BC) invented an ingenious water pump, which became known as Archimedes' screw. It consisted of a tube coiled around a rod, which is set at an angle, with the bottom end in water and a handle at the top. When the handle is rotated, the entire device turns and the tube collects water which is thus transported upwards.

9 Greek Fire

This was the secret weapon of the Byzantine Empire, used against enemy ships. Greek Fire was a highly flammable, jelly-like substance, which was blasted through bronze tubes mounted on the prows of Byzantine galleys, and could not be extinguished by water. It was first employed to repel an Arab fleet attacking Constantinople in 673, and then successfully used in combat until the Empire's fall in 1453. To this day scientists are unsure of its exact formula but think that it probably consisted of liquid petroleum, sulphur, naphtha and quicklime.

10 Pap Smear

Since 1943, cervical cancer has been detected using the Pap smear test, a gynaecological procedure named after its inventor, the Athens-educated Greek-American doctor, George Papanicolaou (1883–1962).

Theatre of Dionysus

Left **Detail of Parthenon frieze by Pheidias** Right **Neo-Classical pediment on the Academy of Arts**

TOP 10 Artistic Styles

1 Cycladic, 3200–2200 BC

The prehistoric Cycladic civilization flourished on the islands of Naxos, Paros, Amorgos, Santorini and Keros (which form a rough circle in the Aegean, hence the name) for 1,000 years before mysteriously disappearing. It left behind hundreds of marble figures: most are elegant, angular, minimalist female figures, probably used in a goddess or fertility cult.

2 Minoan, 2000–1400 BC

The Minoans of Crete were sensual, social, nature-loving and matriarchal. Ceramics are painted with flowing lines based on natural motifs. Fluid-lined frescoes depict priestesses and animals. Most exciting are the faïence sculptures of voluptuous goddesses wielding snakes, and the fantastically light, delicate gold jewellery.

3 Mycenaean, 1500–1300 BC

The art of this martial, mainland culture was somewhat influenced by the Minoans. But fundamentally, they were different, focused on war, order and acquisition, especially of gold. Their palaces housed hoards of embossed-gold swords, daggers, and cups, gold death-masks and pots painted with warrior images.

Female Cycladic figure

4 Geometric, 8th–7th Century BC

Geometric art emerged from a dark age with vases painted with angular designs, and abstract, triangular-rectilinear human forms. The greatest of these is the giant 8th-century BC funerary vase in the National Archaeological Museum, where you can also see the first "Greek key" pattern.

5 Archaic, Late 7th–5th Century BC

The beginning of monumental Greek art, with the first marble temples and sculptures. These earliest sculptures of young men and women, called *koroi*, and made for religious purposes, were heavily influenced by Egyptian art: stiff and still, with muscles and facial features carved mostly as decorations to the form.

6 Classical, 500–320 BC

The Classical movement saw lifelike, naturalistic sculptures, balancing vibrancy and idealism. Temples built according to brilliant mathematical proportions rose, adorned with tradition-shattering sculptural reliefs that seemed to break out from the marble,

The Moschophoru (Calf-Bearer), Archaic period

Hellenistic Bronze head

many created by the sculptor Pheidias, a central figure of Athens' Golden Age.

7 Hellenistic, 320 BC–1st Century AD

Classical sculpture grew ripe and decadent, in part influenced by the new Hellenistic cities in the Orient, part of Alexander the Great's empire. The sculptor Lysippos defined the new phase with sensuous subjects such as Aphrodite, Pan and Dionysus in exaggerated, twisting movement.

8 Byzantine, 324–1453

Byzantine art was almost completely focused on depicting Christian images. Rich, colourful mosaics, frescoes, icons and religious objects were made with valuable materials, especially gold, and intricate, skilfully crafted methods, which conveyed the wealth of the empire.

9 Ottoman Influence, 1453–1821

Under the Turks, cultural activities and art were stifled, but folk arts persisted, incorporating and transforming some aspects from the conqueror's culture, including intricate silver jewellery and metalwork and colourful rugs, tapestries and embroideries.

10 Neo-Classical, 1821–Early 20th Century

After defeating their Ottoman conquerors, Greece began re-building itself, turning to the well-proportioned forms of their great Classical forebears. Many of modern Athens' most important buildings were constructed on this model, notably the University of Athens, the Academy of Athens and the National Library.

Top 10 Artistic Terms

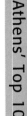

1 Kouros/Kore
The first monumental sculptures in Greek art: a *kouros* was a youth, a *kore* a maiden. The plural is *koroi*.

2 Capital
The top of a column. There are three main Greek forms: Doric, a simple slab; Ionic, a carved scroll; and Corinthian, an acanthus-leaf pattern.

3 Caryatids
Sculptures of women that acted as columns. The most famous are at the Erechtheion at the Acropolis.

4 Pediment
The triangular gable on the façade of a temple where relief sculptures are often carved.

5 Frieze
The horizontal band running below the pediment of a temple, carved with floral, geometric or other decorative motifs.

6 Krater
A large ceramic or bronze bowl for mixing wine and water, often beautifully decorated.

7 Black-Figure
The earliest type of Greek vase-painting: black figures are etched into red ceramic glaze, creating a somewhat stiff, formal image.

8 Red-Figure
A revolutionary method of Classical vase-painting: the outlines of figures are painted on with red glaze, creating flowing, active images.

9 Fresco
A painting made directly into wet plaster, creating art that is one with walls.

10 Icon
Byzantine and Christian images of saints, believed to be imbued with holy power, often painted with gold.

Left **Agora** Centre **Syntagma Metro Station** Right **Kerameikos**

Archaeological Sites

1 Acropolis

If you're only in Athens for a day, this is the one sight to see. The temples, especially the great Parthenon, built to honour Athena, have been the dominating influence in Western architecture for over 2,000 years. They continue to astonish and inspire. *(See pp8–9 and 69.)*

Tower of the Winds

2 New Acropolis Museum

The museum, not yet completed, is being built over a late-Roman and early Byzantine settlement. The site is packed with houses and at least one fountain and reservoir, rare in the parched city. A walkway through the site and glass floors in the museum will allow visitors to see all angles of it, a fascinating juxtaposition to the earlier archaeological finds within the museum. *(See pp10–11 and 69.)*

3 Temple of Olympian Zeus

The colossal temple to Zeus was commissioned in 515 BC and took nearly 700 years to complete, during which time many other buildings – temples, baths and a law court – sprang up around it. *(See pp32–3.)*

4 Syntagma Metro Station

In the late 1990s, Athens undertook its biggest archaeological dig ever: excavating a long-delayed metro – essential for hosting the Olympics. Many feared that the tightly scheduled dig would endanger what lay beneath. The Syntagma metro station was a brilliant compromise: though modern and gleaming, one glass wall looks directly on to the site, with detailed explanations of its ancient layers. *(See p95.)*

5 Roman Forum and Tower of the Winds

One of the most interestingly layered sites. Buildings and remains include the ingenious Tower of the Winds from 50 BC, the first-century AD Roman forum, and a mosque built by the Ottomans. *(See pp20–21.)*

Herodes Atticus Theatre, the Acropolis

6 Hadrian's Library

Hadrian built this luxurious Corinthian-columned building in AD 132. Most of the space was actually a showy marble courtyard, with gardens and a pool. There were also lecture rooms, music rooms and a theatre. The library itself was on the east side, where you can see marble slots for manuscript scrolls. *(See p80.)*

7 Agora

The Agora, the marketplace where philosophers held forth, tradesmen bickered and statesmen hammered out the terms of the first democracy, was the city's heart and soul for 600 years. This is one of the most hands-on sites in Athens and includes the Temple of Hephaestus, the best-preserved ancient Greek temple. *(See pp12–13.)*

8 Kerameikos

This fascinating site around ancient Athens' walls should not be missed. It contains evidence of all the activities that take place at a city's edge: tombs (raised circular mounds for war heroes, pompous marble statues for great statesmen), temples, important roads, pottery workshops, and a brothel. It's also a shady oasis in the congested city centre. *(See pp26–7.)*

9 Kesariani

This 11th-century monastery on the cypress-clad slopes of Mount Hymettos makes a wonderful day trip (best reached by car). The chapel, dedicated to the Presentation of the Virgin, is built atop Classical ruins, its

Temple of Poseidon

walls decorated with cloisonné (enamelled) masonry and late 17th-century paintings. The ram's-head fountain is said to cure infertility. *(See p49.)* ◎ Map T2 • 210 723 6619 • 8:30am–3pm Tue–Sun

10 Temple of Poseidon

The great marble shrine to the sea god, situated on Cape Sounio's peak and surrounded by the Aegean Sea, is among the most stunning sights in all of Greece. It was built in the 5th century BC. British poet Lord Byron was one of many who fell under its spell 2,400 years later, composing poetry in its honour and carving his name on a pillar. Come at sunset, just before it closes, for a spectacular and unforgettable view. ◎ 70 km (44 miles) south of Athens on the Sounio Road • Map T3 • 2292 039 363 • 9am–sunset daily • Adm

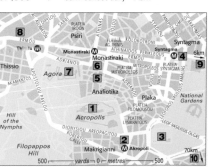

Left **View from the new Acropolis Museum** Centre **Benaki Museum shop** Right **War Museum**

Museums

1 National Archaeological Museum

One of the world's most important museums, jam-packed with a jaw-dropping array of treasures from the ancient and Classical Greek civili-

National Archaeological Museum

zations. Don't miss the exquisite frescoes of 17th-century BC Thira, and the golden hoard of splendid prehistoric Mycenae. *(See pp16–17.)*

2 Agora Museum

The fascinating displays of finds from the city's ancient marketplace focus on objects used in the workings of the first democracy, including the declaration inscribed on marble that a government of democracy, not tyranny, was to rule. *(See pp14–15.)*

3 Museum of Greek Musical Instruments

Greek musical instruments are far more varied than the bouzouki

Agora Museum

that plucked out the theme to *Zorba the Greek*. The Greek musical tradition, though heavily influenced by Turkey and Asia, has filtered through the unique Hellenic sensibility. The array of beautiful instruments includes carved Byzantine lyres, ivory lutes and gypsy flutes. *(See p70.)*

4 New Acropolis Museum

Scheduled to open in early 2008, this beautifully designed museum is being built partly to give a fitting new home to the famed marble sculptures of the Acropolis, and partly as a political gambit to force Britain to return the Parthenon marbles, which currently reside in the British Museum. *(See pp10–11.)*

5 Museum of Greek Folk Art

A rich collection of Greek folk art from 1650 to the present day, including traditional tapestries, embroideries, costumes, shadow puppets, and not-to-be-missed sumptuous filigreed jewellery. Another highlight is an original room full of frescoes by internationally renowned folk artist Theofilos Khatzmikhail, transported in its entirety from his home on the island of Lesvos. *(See p70.)*

Benaki Museum
Follow the progress of Greek art and culture through this first-rate collection from the eras of antiquity to the mid-20th century. Walk through excellently present-ed displays in the gorgeous Neo-Classical mansion of the Benaki family. *(See pp22–3.)*

Museum of Cycladic Art
The Cycladic island civilization of the Aegean flourished at the same time as the early Egyptians and Mesopotamians, but produced something very different: strangely elegant, stylized marble goddess-cult figurines. These were the first pieces in the centuries-long tradition of Greek art that was to follow; this is the world's largest collection. *(See pp18–19.)*

Byzantine Museum
Yet another of the top museums in the world. The Byzantine Museum owns over 15,000 objects from the greatest Byzantine churches and monas-teries worldwide, including sculpture, manuscripts, icons, frescoes and precious, eye-strainingly intricate gold, silver and gem-encrusted ecclesiasti-cal objects. *(See pp28–9.)*

War Museum
A lengthy display of warfare in Greece, beginning with pre-historic battle-axes, running through Alexander the Great's battle plans and the

Byzantine Museum

Greek War of Independence to the present. The Saroglos collection includes medieval swords, Renaissance foils and duelling pistols, engraved Turkish scimitars and samurai blades. Unfortunately, accompanying information is scarce and only in Greek. *(See pp96–7.)*

National Gallery of Art
Greece's most important art gallery, showing the greatest works of Greek artists. Master-pieces by El Greco (known in his homeland by his true name, Domenikos Theotokopoulos) are the highlight of the collection. Hosts major travelling exhibitions.
🔎 *Vas Konstantinou 50 • Map F4 • 9am–3pm Mon & Wed–Sat, 10am–2pm Sun • Adm*

Left **Panagia Grigoroussa** Right **Agios Georgios**

Churches

1 Mitropoli

Athens' massive cathedral of 1862 was the first major church built after Greece's independence. It became the seat of the archbishop and hence of modern Greek orthodoxy. Though its colourful frescoes and pricey ecclesiastical objects are certainly impressive, its architecture is less so. Mitropoli's importance is almost entirely spriritual, as the central point for the Greek Orthodox Church. *(See also p70.)*

2 Panagia Gorgoepikoos

Dwarfed by the bulk of Mitropoli, tiny Panagia Gorgoepikoos (Mikri Mitropoli, "little Mitropoli") actually far outshadows its vast neighbour in historic and artistic importance. It was built in the 12th century, on the ruins of an ancient temple dedicated to goddess Eileithyia. Its walls are built entirely of Roman and Byzantine marble relics, sculpted with reliefs depicting the ancient calendar of feasts. *(See also Mitropoli entry on p70.)*

3 Kapnikarea

This lovely little church, dedicated to the Virgin Mary, was built in the 11th century over the ruins of an ancient temple. It is laid out in the typical Byzantine cross-in-square plan, with three apses on the

Mitropoli looming over Panagia Gorgoepikoos in the foreground

east side and a narthex (a western portico) on the west. Inside, the church is decorated with medieval mosaics. *(See pp80–81.)*

4 Monistiraki

This was once the greatest monastery of the area, this is the church from which the Monistiraki neighbourhood takes its name. "Little monastery" was so named after the destruction of its many surrounding buildings during 19th-century archaeological digs. Restoration of the church was completed in 2007. *(See p80.)*

Kapnikarea

5 Panagia Grigoroussa

If you've lost something or are looking for someone, this is the place to go. Every Saturday, this famous church holds services blessing tasty *fanouropita* cakes. Once eaten, they are supposed to help you find what you're looking for.

Agia Ekaterini

🔊 *By Tower of the Winds • Map J4 • Services Apr–Oct: 5:45pm; Nov–Mar: 4:45pm*

6 Agias Apostoli

This is one of Athens' oldest churches, built in the early 11th century over a 2nd-century monument in the ancient Agora. Though it underwent a great deal of damage during the Ottoman occupation, the remains of its frescoes have been preserved and restored within. 🔊 *Map J4*

7 Agia Ekaterini

Remnants of Classical columns remain in the courtyard of this beautiful 12th-century church – evidence that it too was built over the ruins of an ancient temple, this one possibly dedicated to the goddess Hestia. The church's many colourful frescoes have been lovingly restored. *(See p72.)*

8 Agios Georgios

Claiming the highest point in modern-day Athens – the peak of Lykavittos Hill – Agios Georgios boasts views as far as the Saronic Gulf, the island of Aegina and the Peloponnese coast. Services are held both inside and outside.
Lykavittos Hill • Map P1

9 Dafni

Built in the 6th century, this beautiful monastery church has been used in the course of its life as a prison, insane asylum and army barracks, as well as a revered place of worship. And, like so many churches in and around Athens, its foundations rest upon an ancient temple, this one to Apollo. The magnificent mosaics and awesome vaulted dome are being restored, and the church is hoping to reopen in 2008. *(See p111.)*

10 Kesariani, Mount Hymettos

This 12th-century monastery sits on fragrant, wooded slopes just outside Athens. Most of its surviving frescoes are from the 16th and 17th centuries, and its rushing spring waters are said to cure infertility. *(See p45.)*

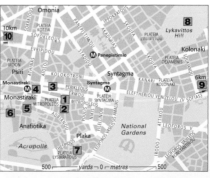

Left **Dionisiou Areopagitiou** Centre **National Gardens** Right **Acropolis from Filopappos Hill**

🔟 City Strolls

1 Dionisiou Areopagitiou Walkway

This wide, tree-lined walkway provides a continuous pedestrian link between all the major archaeological sites in central Athens, and has several open-air cafés.

The open-air theatre on Lykavittos Hill

2 National Gardens

The winding paths of the lush National Gardens are a great place to stroll. In 1839, when this was a royal park, the landscape was densely planted with 15,000 exotic trees and flowers imported from around the world; many of those original plants still flourish. *(See p95.)*

3 Lykavittos Hill

Several pleasant footpaths run through pine-clad Lykavittos Hill. If you're feeling energetic, hike to the top; if climbing's not for you, take the funicular up and saunter down, stopping at the café for a drink. *(See p97.)*

View from Strefi Hill

4 Kallidromiou and Strefi Hill

Kallidromiou is the heart of Exarcheia, especially on Saturdays, when the whole neighbourhood turns out for the open-air *laiki* (farmer's market). Soak up the sights of the street and buy some fresh fruit before heading to nearby Strefi Hill *(p90)* for a healthy climb and bite to eat.

5 Pasalimani

This natural harbour at Piraeus is full of local fishing boats and yachts. Stroll around the marina, ending up on the east side, in front of the Nautical Museum, or come after dark when the many waterside cafés come to life. *(See p103.)*

6 Filopappos Hill

Follow the winding paths to different monuments: two Byzantine churches, a Roman memorial and Athens' old observatory. And, at the summit of this shady hill, extensive views over and beyond the city. *(See pp30–31.)*

Previous pages Antiques market stalls around Ermou

Pediou tou Areos

7 Kallimarmaro Stadium
Fourth-century BC Panathen-aic athletes and the runners of the first modern Olympics in 1896 ran laps in the sweltering centre of this beautiful marble stadium. Modern joggers and walkers love the shady path on top of the 70,000-seat edifice. *(See p95.)*

8 Pediou tou Areos
Athens' largest park is a good retreat on blistering city days. Older people crowd the benches while children play soccer around the statues. As you leave, go through the walkway lined with busts of Greece's War of Independ-ence heroes. *(See p89.)*

9 Ermou
The shopping street. Start at the top, with designer boutiques and department stores, then make your way down to the funkier end, most obviously when Sunday's flea market *(p80)* fills the street. Beyond it are loads of quirky used-furniture, antique and speciality shops.

10 First National Cemetery of Athens
Take a contemplative walk through the wide, overgrown rows of handsome mausoleums in Athens' largest cemetery. It is thickly planted with cypress trees, whose tall, pointed shape Greeks believe helps guide souls up to heaven. 🕲 *Map D–E6*

Top 10 City Views

1 Orizontes Restaurant
Watch the glittering night-time cityscape from Orizontes on Lykavittos Hill. *(See p101.)*

2 Filopappos Monument
Spectacular views directly across to the temples of the Acropolis or to Piraeus and the coast. *(See p30.)*

3 Areopagos
This high, slippery rock jutting over the Agora is where, for centuries, Athens' ruling council met.

4 Adrianou, Monastiraki
Sit in one of the many out-door cafés lining this street for a ring-side view of the ancient marketplace. *(See p82.)*

5 Pil Poule
A romantic restaurant *(see p84)* that's perfect for a view of the Acropolis by moonlight.

6 Galaxy Bar
A popular spot for the fashionable set, the bar on the top floor of the Hilton Hotel offers stunning views over Athens *(see p141).*

7 Strefi Hill
In the shadow of Lykavittos, this green hill *(p90)* is perfect if you desire a shorter climb but comparable views.

8 Athens Tower
Greece's tallest building; no observation deck, but great views if you're visiting any of its companies. 🕲 *Mesogeion ?*

9 Kesariani Monastery
Lovely monastery on the wooded slopes of Mount Hymettos, above Athens' northern suburbs. *(See p45.)*

10 Mount Penteli
Up by the National Observa-tory in the most northerly sub-urb of Athens, you get a great view of the city by day, but an even better one at night.

Left **Loumidis Coffee Shop** Right **Kori**

🔟 Places to Shop

Christoforos Kotentos

One of the hottest young stars to burst onto the Greek fashion scene in recent years, Kotentos's designs are snapped up as fast as he can create them by an adoring clientele of Greece's A-list celebrities and socialites. Purchase one of his inspirational creations from his atelier. ✒ *4th floor, Sachtouri 3, Psiri • Map B3 • 210 325 5434 or 210 325 5156*

Athens' Flea Market

A sprawling and varied market, and if you have an eye for an authentic antique you can pick up outstanding bargains at this Sunday market. Wake up early though – there's not much point arriving here after 11am as the streets become jam-packed

Athens' Flea Market

and most of the treasures disappear quickly. *(See p80.)*

Loumidis

The oldest remaining coffee roaster in Greece. This caffeine-fancier's paradise stocks a wealth of traditional Greek and Turkish coffees, plus all the paraphernalia necessary for its preparation. It also sells a range of beans from around the world, as well as espresso machines, cups, shakers and all the accoutrements one could possibly desire for that perfect cup of coffee. *(See p91.)*

Tsitouras Collection

Finest quality glasses, ornaments, towels, plates, cutlery, bed linen, silk scarves, ties and ashtrays – every piece embellished with the omnipresent gold laurel wreath. The epitome of overstated luxury. ✒ *Solonos 80; Map M1• D Kyriakou 7, Kifissia; Map T2*

Kori

Bringing a new quality to the words souvenir shop, Kori stocks an eclectic mix of accessories and ornaments by some of Greece's brightest and best young artists, as well as replicas of museum pieces and traditional pottery, icons and statuettes. ✒ *Mitropoleos 13 • Map L3*

Karavan

A tiny treasure trove of all that is sinful but irresistibly sweet, Karavan sells quite simply

Zoumboulakis Gallery

the best baklava and kataifi in town. ⊛ *Voukourestiou 11 • Map M2*

Zoumboulakis Gallery

An Athenian institution, this shop showcases the works of both up-and-coming and well established Greek artists. Signed and numbered silkscreens are reasonably priced. ⊛ *Kriezotou 7 • Map M3 • 210 363 4454*

Elena Votsi

With three years' of work for Gucci under her belt, Elena Votsi is now making international waves with her own distinctive pieces. Items from her latest collections are currently available in London, Paris and New York, but the full range can be viewed at her boutique in Athens. Working mainly with gold, lapis lazuli, coral, amethyst and aquamarine, Votsi's trademarks are her thickset, rough-cut necklaces and knuckle-duster rings. ⊛ *Xanthou 7 • Map N/P2*

Lena Katsanidou – Where to Wear

Greece is famous for its leather goods, and no one designs them better than talented young Lena Katsanidou. Her sought-after heavy hide belts, breathtaking (literally) corsets and directional bags all from the softest, quality skins are available from the designer's funky Kolonaki boutique, along with her signature one-shoulder satin tops, inspirational jewellery and a whole host of one-off high-fashion garments. ⊛ *Alopekis 17 & Loukianou • Map P2/3*

Korres

The humble origins of this natural-based, environmentally- and animal-friendly cosmetics brand that is taking Europe and the United States by storm lie in this small homeo-pathic pharmacy. The full collection of haircare, suncare, face and body lotions is available here at very reasonable prices. Delight the senses with refreshing citrus body water spray, the sweetly spicy coriander shower gel or the orange blossom facial cleanser. Being a chemist, this shop is closed on Saturdays (as well as Monday and Wednesday afternoons, like many other shops). ⊛ *Eratosthenous & Ivikou • Map P5*

Karavan

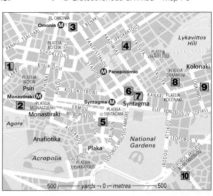

Left **Pil Poule** Right **Beau Brummel**

Restaurants

1 Spondi
Regularly the critics' choice for Athens' best restaurant, Spondi offers faultless cooking. Try sea bass with rose petal and vanilla sauce, and don't skip their wildly adventurous desserts, such as lotus filled with mandarin sorbet on a bed of banana-pineapple purée, with candied olives, vanilla-scented olive oil, and sauce of basil, saffron and curry – magnificent. ✪ *Pyrronos 5 • Map E6 • 210 752 0658 • €€€€*

2 Vardis
Michelin-starred Vardis sets the standard for formal dining in Athens, with a classic French menu and impeccable service. Dishes like veal with caramelized endive and orange are showy but perfect. Dine in the poolside garden in summer. ✪ *Deligianni 66, Pentelikon Hotel, Kifissia • Map T2 • 210 623 0650 • Closed Sun & Aug • €€€€€*

3 To Varoulko
Relocated from Piraeus to Gazi in 2005, To Varoulko is widely acknowledged for serving the best seafood in Athens. Chef Lefteris Lazarou has been awarded a Michelin star. *(See p84.)*

4 Beau Brummel
Former chef at Vardis, Franco-Cretan Jean de Grylleau has brought his talents to a new address. Dishes like soy-citrus

marinated sea bream with cold tagliatelle are refined but bursting with flavour, and an excellent wine list boasts the best from Greece and France. ✪ *Agiou Dimitriou 9, Kifissia • Map T2 • 210 623 6780 • €€€€*

5 Etrusco
Chef Ettore Bottrini and his Italian wife Monica have brought their successful restaurant from Corfu to the splendid roof garden of the Athenian Carllirhoe Hotel. Highlights of the menu include a delicate terrine of white chocolate and fresh peaches. *(See p75.)*

6 48 The Restaurant
With its polished concrete walls and floor, water garden and coloured lighting, 48 has become one of the trendiest restaurants in town. ✪ *Armatolon & Klefton 48, Ambelokipi • Map F2 • 210 641 1082 • €€€€*

7 Milos
Costas Spiliades, who founded New York's highly acclaimed Estiatorio Milos, has

Pil Poule

48 The Restaurant

opened a sister restaurant in Athens' Hilton Hotel. Expect exquisite Greek seafood dishes, a luxurious setting and impeccable service. ◈ *Hilton Hotel, Vasilissis Sofias 46 • Map G4 • 210 728 1000 • €€€€*

8 Edodi

No menu at this tiny gem, just raw ingredients to choose and have cooked to order. Edodi is noted for delicate flavours and unexpected sauces, creating delights like fig-stuffed pheasant and lobster with parmesan sauce. *(See p75.)*

9 Orizontes

Perched on Lykavittos Hill, Orizontes is an unforgettable dining venue. The city views are stunning and the creative Mediterranean cuisine and extensive wine list are both excellent. *(See p101.)*

10 Pil Poulc

The view of the Acropolis by moonlight is reason enough to come here, but exquisite food and flawless service elevate the experience to sublime. Dishes like lobster with mango and champagne, sea bream stuffed with lime, and fried strawberries with chocolate live up to the heady ambience. *(See p84.)*

Top 10 Tavern

1 Karavitis
Cumin-flavoured (meatballs) and tzatzik that steps back in time *nou & Pafsaniou • Map*

2 Mamacas
Classic taverna fare in the revitalized industrial district. A celebrity favourite. ◈ *Persephonis 41, Gazi • €*

3 Filipou
Old-world taverna in Athens' poshest neighbourhood. ◈ *Xenokratous 19 • Map F3 • €*

4 Bakaliarakia tou Damigou
A 100-year-old-plus underground hideaway with justly famous fried cod and its very own ancient column. *(See p75.)*

5 Vlassis
An Athenian favourite for generations; exemplary mezes. ◈ *Pasteur 8 & Platcia Mavili • Closed summer • €*

6 Skoufias
Inspired by Greek and Cretan influences the best dish on the menu is the delicious pork *kotsi*. *(See p92.)*

7 Strofi
Traditional favourites and tasty updates in a garden rooftop setting with stunning Acropolis view. *(See p75.)*

8 Psaras
One of the few unspoiled garden tavernas in Plaka. ◈ *Erectheos 16 & Erotokritiou • Man K4 • €*

9 Frantzescos
Spicy Asia-minor flavoured treats in leafy Kifissia. ◈ *Skiathou 3, Kifissia • Map T2 • €*

10 Monopoleio Athinon
Light and modern taverna fare, often with live rembetika at weekends. ◈ *Ippothontidon & Kiriadon, Kato Petralona • Closed summer • €*

Left **Barba Yannis restaurant (see p92)** Centre **Gemista** Right **Fassolada**

🔟 Greek Dishes

1 Grilled Octopus
Best caught and served on the same day, having been grilled over hot coals, topped with a squeeze of lemon and drizzled with oil and vinegar. The texture should be tender and the taste salty-sweet.

Moussaka

2 Moussaka
There are endless variations on this famous country casserole. But the basic ingredients – aubergine (eggplant) and minced lamb layered with potatoes and tomatoes, enriched with wine, spiced with cinammon and topped with bechamel – stay the same, as does its warming, earthy flavour.

3 Pittes
Pittes came to Greece from Turkey and the Middle East. The key to a perfect *pita* (which means "pie") is the famous filo crust: dozens of layers of paper-thin, translucent dough, brushed with butter or olive oil and baked to light, flaky perfection. *Pita* fillings range from sweet (the honey, walnut and rosewater baklava) to savoury – spinach and feta or *hortopita*, made from wild greens.

4 Stifado
This rich, tender wild rabbit stew comes from the mountains of northern Greece, where it still

Souvlaki

warms villagers every winter. The rabbit is spiced with cumin, cloves and cinnamon, but its most wonderful characteristic is an unusual sweetness, achieved by the addition of lots of small onions, cooked until caramelized.

5 Horiatiki
A bastardized version appears on menus worldwide as "Greek salad". The real thing is just a matter of fresh ingredients. Sun-ripened tomatoes, crisp cucumbers, crunchy red onions and green peppers, rich Kalamata olives, topped by a slab of feta, aromatic oregano and extra-virgin olive oil make up this simple but halcyon salad.

6 Souvlaki
Souvla means spit-roasted, and this is the Greeks' favourite way to serve meat. *Souvlaki* refers to the ubiquitous street favourite: hunks of chicken, pork or lamb spit-roasted for hours, slathered with tzatziki, and stuffed along with onions and tomatoes into a hot, freshly baked, oiled and fried bread-dough.

7 Gemista
Gemista simply means "stuffed". Greeks stuff tomatoes, aubergines, courgettes (zucchini), peppers and

Pittes

vine leaves with all manner of ingredients, including rice, herbs, mince, raisins, pine nuts and an array of spices. Often topped with a creamy, lemony sauce, *gemista* make a fulfilling meal on their own.

8 Fassolada
The staple winter dish for the ancient Greeks, *fassolada* is still Greece's most popular soup. White beans, carrots, onions, tomatoes and oregano are simmered in stock until tender, then topped with the crucial ingredient: extra-virgin olive oil. In summer, cold *fassolada* is often served as a meze in the afternoon.

9 Kokoretsi
New EU food laws have made this essential Easter dish technically illegal, but in back gardens and old-time tavernas Greeks continue to serve it year round. They take the intestines of lamb, marinate them in herbs, garlic and lemon juice, and roast the whole thing for hours over coals, until it drips with flavourful juices.

10 Kokkinisto
This is a simple, classic taverna dish, whose name means "red-sauced". Lamb, chicken or pork is cooked with tomatoes, wine and herbs in a clay pot, which keeps in all the moisture and pungent flavour. The tender, infused meat should fall off the bone at the mere touch of a fork.

Top 10 Greek Drinks

1 Ouzo
Greece wouldn't be the same without this spirit. Drunk with mezes, this aniseed flavoured distillate packs a powerful punch.

2 Tsipouro
Made from the residue left after distilling muscatel grapes, fiery, warming *tsipouro* does its job best in winter months.

3 Retsina
Not subtle, but affection for this wine with pine resin cuts across all age and class barriers.

4 Hima
Home-made barrel wine, often poured into pitchers or plastic bottles directly from casks on the taverna wall.

5 Mavrodaphne
It means "black laurel". The best grapes for this rich, dark, port-like sweet wine come from the Peloponnese.

6 Aghiorghitiko
Deep, velvety "St George" wines from Nemea are the rising stars of the growing Greek wine industry.

7 Assyrtiko
Greece's finest white wine is redolent of honeysuckle and figs – one of the most unusual in the Mediterranean.

8 Savatiano
Greece's most common white wine is great with seafood and salads; it's most often found in tavernas.

9 Greek Coffee
Thick, sweet, pungent mud of strong, black coffee. Ask for an *elliniko metrio*.

10 Frappé
Nescafé, milk and cold water whipped into a pleasant, cool froth.

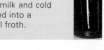

Left **Lykavittos Festival** Right **Independence Day**

🔟 Festivals and Events

Easter feast of roast lamb

Epiphany (6 Jan)
The "Blessing of the Waters", when ports, boats and beaches are blessed, and young men dive for crosses cast into the water by priests; it's a year's good luck for the successful divers.

Apokries (Feb–Mar)
The Greek Orthodox Carnival begins 58 days before Easter. Festivities, especially glamorous masquerade parties, last for days. In Athens, the colourful celebrations centre on Plaka, where the streets are packed with celebrants and masked musicians.

Clean Monday
Greeks celebrate the first day of Lent by going to the country and flying kites; in Athens, the sky above Filopappos Hill is usually filled with them.

Independence Day (25 Mar)
Full-on military parades with tanks, guns and battalions celebrate the date in 1821 when, after nearly 400 years of occupation, the Greek revolution successfully rose up against the Ottoman Empire.

Easter
The most important event on the Orthodox calendar, far outweighing Christmas. On the night of Easter Friday, participants follow effigies of Jesus on flower-covered biers in candlelit processions, concluding in midnight services and exuberant fireworks (and, in mountain villages, rounds of gunshots). Sunday is for roasting lamb with 20–30 close family members and eating eggs dyed red (symbolizing both the blood of Christ and rebirth).

Hellenic Festival (Jun–Sep)
Ancient Greeks performed their timeless tragedies in the spectacular theatres of Herodes Atticus and Epidauros. Now, every summer, the world's greatest singers, dancers and

Hellenic festival at Epidauros

actors perform under moonlight in these world-renowned venues. Recent singers include Luciano Pavarotti and the Harlem Gospel Choir, while Gerard Depardieu and Isabella Rossellini have acted in performances of classical works at Epidauros. ✎ www.greekfestival.gr

Lykavittos Festival (Jun–Sep)
Top music acts such as Bob Dylan, Phillip Glass and BB King perform in the theatre nestled at the steep peak of Lykavittos Hill. ✎ www.greekfestival.gr

Rockwave (Jun)
This three-day festival is Greece's hottest music ticket of the year. The line-up includes huge Greek and international pop, rock and alternative acts. ✎ www.rockwavefestival.gr

Feast of the Virgin (15 Aug)
Absolutely everything closes for the Assumption of the Virgin, which is second only to Easter in the Orthodox calendar. The full cross-section of Greek womanhood packs churches, as every "Maria" turns out to honour her namesake.

Athens Marathon (early Nov)
Athletes from around the world retrace the course of Pheidippidis, antiquity's most celebrated runner. In 490 BC, the Greeks defeated the Persians at Marathon in a historic battle for democracy (see p124). Pheidippidis ran the 42 km (26 miles) to Athens, announced the outcome ("Victory!"), then died of exhaustion. Today's runners have the advantage of water stops and cheering crowds en route from Marathonas to the Kallimarmaro Stadium (see p95) to ease the arduous feat.

Top 10 Saints' Days

St Basil (1 Jan)
Families eat Vasilopita (Basil's cake), into which coins have been baked. Finding a coin brings a year's good luck.

St John the Baptist (7 Jan)
The day John baptized Christ in the Jordan river. Various regional traditions involve dunking local men in water.

St Athanassios (18 Jan)
Today the church auctions off donated gifts in honour of Athanassios, one of Orthodoxy's three holy Fathers.

St Charalambos (10 Feb)
An important day for hospitals in Greece, who today honour the patron saint of physicians.

St George (23 Apr)
The dragon-slayer is the patron saint of the military, who honour him today.

St Dimitrios (26 Oct)
The greatest celebrations are in Thessaloniki, where this martyr, whose wounds ran with myrrh instead of blood, is patron saint.

St Catherine (25 Nov)
This famous martyr is honoured as the protectress of infants, maidens and students.

St Stelianos (26 Nov)
Pregnant women stay home from work to ask Stelianos, patron of infants and childbirth, to protect their children.

St Barbara (4 Dec)
Mothers sometimes make their children sleep in a church on the night of St Barbara to protect them from illness.

St Nicholas (6 Dec)
Celebrations in honour of the patron saint of sailors are especially festive on islands and in coastal areas.

Left **Olympic flag** Centre **Architect Santiago Calatrava** Right **Athens Olympic Complex, Maroussi**

⟶10 Olympic Venues

1 Athens Olympic Sports Complex

This was the Games' central attraction. The existing multi-stadium complex was expanded and renovated to host the opening and closing ceremonies, plus tennis, gymnastics, basketball finals, swimming, diving, water polo and cycling. Spanish architect Santiago Calatrava designed the glass and steel stadium domes. There are plans to transform the surrounding area into a verdant art-filled park. ⊗ *Kifissias, Maroussi*

Olympic sign

2 Goudi Olympic Complex

This complicated building hosted the pentathlon. It includes a 2,000-seat area for swimming, two 5,000-seat areas for riding and running and one 4,500-seat area for fencing and shooting. A temporary 5,000-seat area also hosted badminton. ⊗ *Katechaki, Goudi*

3 Kallimarmaro Stadium

This showpiece in central Athens was built in the 4th century BC for the Panathenaic Games. It later fell into disuse, but was restored with beautiful Pentelic marble for the first modern Olympics in 1896. In 2004, it hosted archery and the Marathon finish. ⊗ *Vasileos Konstantinou*

4 Olympic Weight-Lifting Hall

Weightlifting is Greece's most successful international sport – the team bagged five medals in Sydney. The lifting arena was one of the first Olympic venues planned for 2004, and organizers claimed that the 5,000-seat hall was the biggest venue ever built for showcasing weightlifting. ⊗ *Ralli Petrou, Nikaia*

5 Faliron Coastal Zone Olympic Complex

The beachside Peace and Friendship Stadium, which seats 14,000 spectators, hosted volleyball. Two coastal sports pavilions – one seating 10,000, the other 8,000 – hosted boxing, handball and Tae Kwon Do (an extremely popular sport among Greeks). Two sandy beach volleyball courts

Kallimarmaro Stadium

Part of Athens Olympic Sports Complex

provided seating for 10,000 and 4,000. 🕈 *Faliron*

6 Hellenikon Sports Complex

This massive complex is on the site of Athens' former airport, converted for 2004 into major sports facilities. It hosted basketball, baseball, softball, fencing, handball, hockey and canoe slalom. There are plans to convert the complex into a giant park which could be the largest in Europe. Though some land will be sold to developers to fund the project. 🕈 *Poseidonos*

7 Olympic Sailing Centre

The sailing centre was the first Olympic venue to host a test event – an international regatta in 2002. Sailing events were among the most exciting competitions of the whole games, partly because of the *meltemi* winds, which gust reliably along the coast every August. There are plans to convert the site into a 1,170-berth marina. 🕈 *Agios Kosmas*

8 Markopoulo Olympic Equestrian Centre

Everything horsey was here, with stables for 300 horses. Construction

on this centre was delayed when archaeologists uncovered a shrine to goddess Aphrodite. Post Games there are plans to build an 18-hole golf course on the site.

9 Olympic Canoe and Rowing Centre

Canoeing and rowing competitions took place in a 2,200-m (7,300-ft) artificial lake, with seating for 14,000 spectators. Now there are plans to make the area an environmental zone, with an adjoining archaeological park, displaying Stone-Age finds uncovered during construction and finds from the nearby site of the Battle of Marathon *(see p124)*. 🕈 *Schinias, Marathonas*

10 Acharnes Olympic Mountain Bicycling Venue

The cycling and mountain bike competitions were held along a magnificent route on Mount Parnitha, a stunning area of natural beauty just outside Athens, frequently overlooked by visitors. 🕈 *Mount Parnitha*

Left **Puppet theatre** Right **Maria Callas**

Moments in the History of Theatre and Music

1 The Rites of Dionysus, 1200–600 BC

Annual rites to the god of wine and revelry were held each spring, and involved orgies, feasts and the ingestion of herbs that led to wild ecstasies. A dithyramb (ode to Dionysus) was sung by a chorus of men dressed as satyrs. It eventually evolved into narratives, which in turn developed into the first plays.

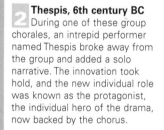

Dionysus

2 Thespis, 6th century BC

During one of these group chorales, an intrepid performer named Thespis broke away from the group and added a solo narrative. The innovation took hold, and the new individual role was known as the protagonist, the individual hero of the drama, now backed by the chorus.

3 Drama Competitions, 534 BC

In 534 BC, the ruler of Athens, Pisistratus, formalized the Dionysan festivals into fully fledged drama competitions, held annually. Thespis won the first competition.

4 Aeschylus, the First Playwright, 472 BC

To the protagonist, Aeschylus introduced a second character, the antagonist, creating new possibilities. Then in 472 BC came *Persians*, the earliest known play.

5 Sophocles Beats Aeschylus in the Drama Competition, 468 BC

Sophocles brought another innovation to the blossoming form of drama – a third character. He also wrote what is still considered the greatest masterpiece of tragedy, *Oedipus Rex*.

6 Greek Shadow Puppet Theatre, 16th Century

After the golden age of Athenian drama, Greece's performing arts stagnated. However, during the Turkish occupation, Greeks drew on an Eastern tradition of shadow puppet theatre. The stylized, colourful spectacles were satirical and bawdy, the main character (the fool Karaghiozis) joking at the expense of his Turkish masters.

7 Rembetika Emerges, 1870s

When the Greeks came out of 400 years of Turkish occupation, one of the first art forms to coalesce was rembetika, a form of music that can be compared, culturally, to the American Blues. Heavily influenced by music and instruments from Asia Minor, rembetika lyrics tell of life's underside: drugs, destitution, erotic love and squalor.

  For more on Greece's early playwrights see pp36–7

8 Maria Callas Dominates Opera, 1950s and 1960s

"La Divina", born Maria Kalogero-poulos, was the original diva. The fiery first lady of opera enraged many managers at La Scala and the Metropolitan with her temperamental whims, but seduced millions, including shipping magnate Aristotle Onassis, with her heavenly soprano and unforgettable gaze.

9 Mikis Theodorakis Writes the Songs of a Generation, 1960s and 1970s

Mikis Theodorakis, Greece's greatest modern composer, won international acclaim and started a cultural revolution in his own country with works like *Epiphania* and the instantly recognizable *Zorba the Greek* score. During the junta, Theodorakis's songs were banned and he was jailed, making him an instant symbol of the resistance.

10 Vangelis's Chariots of Fire, 1981

Greek composer Vangelis won an Academy Award for his memorable score for *Chariots of Fire*, a film about Olympic runners. Vangelis is internationally recognized for his electronic compositions and film scores, and retains superstar status in Greece.

Anthony Quinn in *Zorba the Greek*

Top 10 Venues

1 Herodes Atticus Theatre
Athens' premiere showcase for performing arts for nearly 2,000 years *(p9)*. ✆ *Box office: Panepistimiou 39 • Map L/M2 • 210 322 1459*

2 Stoa Athanaton
Athens' favourite rembetatiko *(p93)*. ✆ *Central Market, Omonia (in the arcade) • Map C3*

3 National Opera
A little moth-eaten, but this place is still beloved by Athenians. ✆ *Akadimias 59–61 • Map L1 • 210 361 2461*

4 National Theatre
Home of the Greek National Theatre Company, whose performances of the classics are renowned. ✆ *Agiou Konstantinou 22 • Map B2 • 210 522 3242*

5 An
Rock, reggae and alternative performances in the heart of Exarcheia *(p93)*.

6 Gagarin
Great musicians often play at this venue. ✆ *Liosion 205, Attiki • Map B1 • 210 854 7600*

7 Megaro Moussikis
Fantastic acoustics for the world's best orchestras, ballets and opera companies. ✆ *Vas Sofias & Kokkali • Map G3 • 210 728 2333–7 • Closed in summer*

8 Lykavittos Theatre
Hillside theatre showcasing top-notch musical acts, from rock to classical *(p97)*.

9 Half Note
Every top jazz musician passing through Athens has played here. ✆ *Trivonianou 17 • Map M6 • 210 921 3310*

10 Epidauros
Only ancient classics are performed in this famous amphitheatre *(p119)*. ✆ *Tickets available from the Herodes Atticus box office*

AROUND ATHENS

BEYOND ATHENS

ATHENS' TOP 10

Left **Fallen column, Temple of Olympian Zeus** Centre **Plaka restaurants** Right **Plaka streets**

Plaka, Makrigianni and Koukaki

THE WINDING MEDIEVAL ALLEYWAYS *of Plaka, the old quarter below the Acropolis, are easily the most charming part of Athens. Naturally, they are also the most visited, and in midsummer some streets can be packed with touts and cheap gift shops. But Plaka is also very good at concealing places of untouched delight. The working-class areas of Makrigianni and Koukaki are shaking off old dust, and must-see museums, four-star restaurants and ultra-hip clubs are appearing.*

Sculptures from the Acropolis

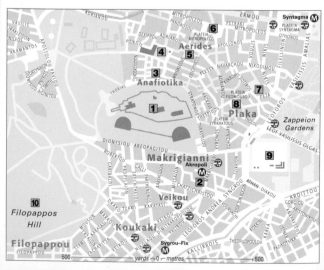

Previous pages **The Theatre at Delphi**

Acropolis
The sacred rock of the Acropolis dominates Plaka, and its different temples are clearly visible from all angles throughout the neighbourhood. Legend holds that it was on this rock that Athena (p39) won dominion of Athens from Poseidon, and it has been devoted to worshipping the goddess since 650 BC. (See also pp8–9 and 44.)

The Parthenon at the Acropolis

New Acropolis Museum
This all-glass $100 million showpiece, designed by internationally renowned architect Bernard Tschumi and opening in early 2008, is meant to give a fitting home to Greece's greatest treasures: the marble sculptures that once adorned the Acropolis, especially the mighty Parthenon. (Until the New Museum opens, these sculptures will still be housed in the small on-site Acropolis museum.) (See also pp10–11, 44 and 46.)

Anafiotika
Clinging to the side of the Acropolis is Athens' loveliest and quirkiest hidden neighbourhood. It was built in the 19th century by tradesmen from the Cycladic island of Anafi, brought to Athens after the War of Independence to build King Otto's palace. They missed home so much that they decided to re-create a pocket of it here, all island-style, dome-topped blue-and-white houses, covered with banks of bougainvillea, in a maze of tiny passageways. Many descendents of the original Anafi workers still live here.

Roman Forum and Tower of the Winds
Julius Caesar and Augustus were founders of this Roman marketplace, which replaced the original Greek Agora, and their names are inscribed on the grand Gate of Athena Archegetis. But its most striking feature, the Tower of the Winds, was built in 50 BC, 100 years earlier. There is no other building like it in the ancient world: eight-sided, each side sculpted with a personification of the winds and their names inscribed: Boreas, Kaikias, Apeliotes, Euros, Notos, Lips, Zephyros and Skiron. (See also pp20–21 and 44.)

Tower of the Winds

Mitropoli

5 Museum of Greek Musical Instruments

This unassuming museum is a great treasure. Here you can see and hear the Middle Eastern and European influences on Greek music, and how Greeks transformed them into something of their own. The instruments themselves are beautiful, often intricately inlaid with silver, ivory and tortoise-shell. It is also an ethno-musicology study centre, and there are occasional courtyard performances. *(See also p46.)* ◈ *Diogenous 1–3 • Map K4 • 210 362 9513 • 10am–2pm Tue & Thu–Sun, noon–6pm Wed • Free*

Museum of Greek Musical Instruments

6 Mitropoli

Enormous, lavishly appointed Athens Cathedral is one of the city's best-known landmarks. The archbishop of Greece (often cited as the nation's most influential person) gives addresses here, and it is regularly packed when Athens' high society come for

Museum of Greek Folk Art

Lord Byron

Among Plaka's many famous residents was Romantic poet and philhellene Lord Byron (1788–1824), who lived in a Capuchin monastery that stood on Plateia Lysikratous, while writing *Childe Harold*. He left to fight on the Greek side in the War of Independence. Athens remembers him in a street off the square named after him: Vyronas, in Greek.

weddings and baptisms. Of far greater artistic importance, though, is tiny Panagia Gorgoepikoos ("little Metropoli"), next door. The 12th-century church is built of Roman and Byzantine marble relics, depicting 90 scenes of ancient feasts. *(See also p48.)* ◈ *Plateia Mitropoleos • Map K3 • 7am–7pm daily • Free*

7 Museum of Greek Folk Art

The dimly lit, government-run building won't win prizes, but inside are five floors packed with rich, beautiful folk art, from jewellery to decorate and cover the entire body to fine embroideries worked with gold and silver thread. There's also a room of wall paintings by primitivist painter Theofilos Khatzmikhail. *(See p46.)* ◈ *Kydathinaion 17 • Map L4 • 10am–2pm Tue–Sun • Limited info in English • Adm*

8 Plateia Filomousou

At some point everyone passes through this green, shady plateia, lined with cafés both old-world and trendy. Try To Tristato for Victorian ambience and heavenly teas and cakes, or Ionos for a view of the scene *(see p74 for both)*. Catch a rooftop movie and Acropolis view at Cine Paris. Relax on benches in the almost-hidden stone-paved centre. Neo-

Classical buildings peer over tree-tops at the whole scene. ◈ *Map L4*

⁹ Temple of Olympian Zeus
All that remains of Greece's largest temple, a shrine to Zeus, is 16 columns. But standing alone, silhouetted by the bright Attic sky, their majesty still overwhelms. Inside the temple was a colossal gold-and-ivory sculpture of the god, a copy of the one at Olympus, which was one of the Seven Wonders of the ancient world. *(See also pp32–3.)*

¹⁰ Filopappos Hill
Next to the parched Acropolis rock, pine-and-cypress-clad Filopappos Hill offers a cool, green place to stroll. The peak is marked by the tomb and monument of Roman senator and philhellene Gaius Julius Antiochus Filopappos, and distinguished by sweeping views from the Acropolis to the sea. In summer, the Dora Stratou Dance Troupe puts on nightly performances of Greek folk dances in a theatre nestled among the pines. *(See also pp30–31.)*

Temple of Olympian Zeus

A Morning in Plaka

Early Morning

🕐 Hike up to the **Acropolis** first thing to beat the heat and the worst of the crowds. Then spend an hour or so admiring the temples.

Come down from the Acropolis and turn left onto the **Dionisiou Areopagitiou walkway** *(see p52)*. Your Acropolis ticket gives you free entry into the **Theatre of Dionysus**, where many of the great Classical dramas were first staged.

Head back out to the walkway and turn right on Makrigianni to visit the **New Acropolis Museum** *(see pp10–11)*. Next, head to Plateia Lysikratous, named after the unusual monument to the winner of a 335 BC choral competition.

🍴 Stop for a frappé in one of the leafy cafés overlooking Lysikratous – O Diogenous has the best view.

Late Morning

From the square, head up towards the charming 19th-century quarter of **Anafiotika** *(see p69)* to explore its twisting alleys.

Leave by Prytaneiou, stopping in the quiet garden of the Byzantine **Church of the Holy Sepulchre**, and lighting a candle from its famed extra-holy flame.

From Prytaneiou, turn right on Mnisikleous and left on Kyrristou for a choice of either the tiny but delightful **Museum of Greek Musical Instruments** or the **Roman Forum and Tower of the Winds** *(see pp20–21)*. Finally, head back a block to **O Platanos** *(see p75)*, for a hefty Greek lunch under a huge plane tree.

Around Athens – Plaka, Makrigianni and Koukaki

Left **Church of Agia Ekaterini** Centre **Children's Art Museum** Right **Jewish Museum**

Best of the Rest

1 Lalaounis Museum
Jeweller Ilias Lalaounis show-cases his gold creations. ◈ *Kallisperi 12 • Map J5 • 9am–4pm Mon & Thu–Sat, 11am–4 pm Sun, 9am–9pm Wed • Adm (free Sat 9–11am, Wed after 3pm)*

2 Kanellopoulos Museum
A miscellany of high-quality antiquities from a family collection, housed in a Neo-Classical mansion. ◈ *Theorias 12 • Map J4 • 8:30am–3pm Tue–Sun • Adm*

3 Church of the Holy Sepulchre
Miracles are associated with this beautiful Byzantine church, and many flock here at Easter to light candles from the holy flame. ◈ *Between Prytaneiou and Erotokritou • Map K4*

4 Study Centre for the Art of Puppet Theatre
Greeks have told funny, subversive tales via shadow puppet theatre for centuries. The art form is kept alive here. ◈ *Tripodon 30 • Map K4 • Performances (in Greek) 11am & 5pm Sun*

5 Choregic Monument of Lysikrates
This cylindrical monument built in 335 BC honours Lysikrates, victor in the Dionysian Choral competition *(see p64)*. ◈ *Pl Lysikratous • Map L5*

6 Church of Agia Ekaterini
This lovely restored Byzan-tine church is on the site of an ancient temple, whose columns still stand below the courtyard. ◈ *Off Plateia Lysikratous • Map L5*

7 Frissiras Museum of Contemporary European Painting
A new, well-run museum of over 3,000 works of top post-war Greek and European artists. ◈ *Monis Asteriou Tsagari 3 & 7 • Map L4 • 210 323 4678 • www.frissirasmuseum. com • 10am–5pm Wed–Fri, 11am–5pm Sat & Sun • Adm*

8 Church of the Holy Trinity
The largest medieval church in Athens, it was built in 1031 and is now Athens' Russian Orthodox church. ◈ *Filellinon • Map L4*

9 Children's Art Museum
Exhibitions showcase work by young artists in mountain tribes, international cities and refugee centres. Many activities for kids. ◈ *Kodrou 9 • Map L4 • 210 331 2621 • Sep–Jul: 10am–2pm Tue–Sat, 11am–2pm Sun • Adm (children free)*

10 Jewish Museum
The collection's 15,000 items tell the story of Jews in Greece. ◈ *Nikis 39 • Map L4 • 210 322 5582 • www.jewishmuseum.gr • 9am–2:30pm Mon–Fri, 10am–2pm Sun • Adm*

Left **Emblem** Centre **O Brettos** Right **Mesogeia**

🔟 Souvenirs and Gifts

1 Centre of Hellenic Tradition
A cavernous warehouse of handicrafts from every corner of the country. If you only have time for one souvenir stop, make this it. ◎ *Mitropoleos 59 • Map K3*

2 Pantelis Mountis
In Pantelis Mountis's hole-in-the-wall, you can purchase beautiful hand-painted icons and metal *tamata* to ward off specific ailments. ◎ *Apollonos 27 • Map L3*

3 Village Flokati
This shop has plenty of Greece's famous hairy *flokatia* rugs, made from woolly mountain sheep. ◎ *Mitropoleos 19 • Map K3*

4 Kori
This tasteful little shop sells a select choice of gifts, including highly individual, signed and numbered artworks by some of the country's latest talents.
◎ *Mitropoleos & Voulis 13 • Map K3*

5 Ilari Galaktozaharoplasteio
The name – which translates as Ilari's dairy and pastry shop – is a mouthful, and so are the delicious traditional Greek sweets sold here. The specialities are old-fashioned puddings.
◎ *Adrianou 112 • Map K3/4*

6 Emblem
Specializing in paintings of ships, this shop sells a variety of handmade crafts including painted trays, wooden taverna signs, worry beads and silver and gold jewellery. ◎ *Makrigianni 15c • Map L4*

7 O Brettos
Pop in for a bottle of this distillery's fiery home-made ouzo, and stay to sip a shot of surprisingly sweet *mestiha* and admire the huge barrels under the eaves *(see p74)*. ◎ *Kydathinaion 41 • Map L4*

8 Mesogeia
This little gem of a grocery shop stocks cheeses from all over the country, olive oil, olives, wine, ouzo, herbs and spices, teas, and some organic goods.
◎ *Nikis 52 & Kydathinaion • Map L4*

9 Lalaounis Museum Jewellery Shop
Some of the world's most glamorous gold creations are still to be found at Ilias Lalounis' celebrated jewellery house. ◎ *Corner of Karyatidon & Kallisperi • Map J5*

10 Sirines
Handmade worry beads, lucky charms, key rings, beaded bracelets and earrings are sold at this small shop. ◎ *Makrigianni 3 • Map K6*

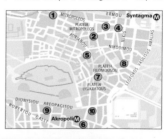

Left **Klepsydra** Centre **Melina** Right **O Brettos**

🔟 Cafés and Bars

1 Klepsydra

This tiny, quiet bar-café behind the Tower of the Winds is surrounded by flower pots and pastel-hued buildings. Locals love it as it's nicely tucked away. ® *Thrasiboulou • Map K4*

2 Melina

This pink-and-gilt shrine to late Greek actress and national heroine Melina Mercouri was once her favourite café. ® *Lyssiou 22, Aerides • Map K4*

3 Galaktopoleion Amaltheia

Stop by this small, cosy spot on a rainy night. The elaborate antique mirrors, old jukebox, huge selection of teas and crackling woodstove will keep you warm. ® *Tripodon 16 • Map K4*

4 O Brettos

The walls here are lined with hundreds of bottles of home-made, brilliantly coloured liquors that glow like stained-glass windows. The drinks are good, too. ® *Kydathinaion 41 • Map L4*

5 Oionos

Though this is the youngest, hippest spot on the square, it's still easy to relax among the ivy-covered outdoor walls. ® *Aggelou Geronta 7, Plateia Filomousou • Map L4*

6 Dioskouri

Hidden away in a corner of Plaka, next to the Agora, this *ouzeri* is popular with local students. Visit for a sunset drink and a platter of mixed appetizers. ® *Dioskoudon 9, Plaka • Map J4*

7 To Tristato

The old-world atmosphere – all potted palms, portraits and pink swags – might almost distract you entirely from the prime reason for coming here: the spectacular pastries and mountain teas. ® *Aggelou Geronta & Daidalou • Map L4*

8 Lamda

Two floors of silver-and-holograph walls, up-to-the-minute Eurotechno music, and model-perfect boy clientele make this one of Athens' hottest gay bars. ® *Lempesi 15 • Map K6*

9 Ionos

A romantic spot for a night-cap, Ionos is open until 1am daily. Coffee and drinks are served at the marble-top tables outside on the leafy square. ® *Geronta 7, Plateia Filomoussou, Plaka • Map L4*

🔟 Vyni

One of Athens' few full beer gardens offers an international range of brews on tap, plus Hellenized pub grub. ® *Drakou 10 • Map C6*

Recommend your favourite bar on traveldk.com

Price Categories

For a three-course meal for one with half a bottle of wine (or equivalent meal), taxes and extra charges.

€ under €30
€€ €30–€40
€€€ €40–€50
€€€€ €50–€60
€€€€€ over €60

Left **O Platanos** Right **Eden**

🔟 Restaurants and Tavernas

1 O Platanos
Amid Plaka's tourist traps, O Platanos's tender, aromatic lamb and home-made retsina have been classics since 1932. ◈ Diogenous 4 • Map K4 • 210 322 0666 • Closed Sun • No credit cards • €

2 Eden
Greece's first vegetarian restaurant opened in 1982 and is still a haven for herbivores. The atmosphere is refreshingly bright and non-hippie. ◈ Lyssiou 12, Aerides • Map K4 • 210 324 8858 • No credit cards • €

3 Scholiarhio
Though somewhat touristy these days, this ouzeri still radiates character. Pick from the daily offerings on a tray. ◈ Tripodon 14 • Map K4 • 210 324 7605 • No credit cards • €

4 Eat at Milton's
The sleek, minimalist decor might be at odds with quaint Plaka, but the Mediterranean cuisine suits the area perfectly. There is occasional live jazz.
◈ Adrianou 91, Plaka • Map K4 • 210 324 9129 • €€

5 Bakaliarakia tou Damigou
The name means "codfish", which this local favourite has been serving up, with garlic sauce, for 140 years. ◈ Kydathinaion 41 (basement) • Map L4 • 210 322 5084 • Closed Mon • No credit cards • €

6 Daphne's
If there's a celebrity in town, they're sure to eat in the frescoed dining room of this Neo-Classical mansion. ◈ Lysikratous 4 • Map L5 • 210 322 7971 • €€€

7 Etrusco
For a special night out, book a table on the roof terrace with splendid views over the Acropolis. ◈ Athenian Callirhoe Hotel, Kallirois 32 & Petmeza • Map C6 • 210 921 5353 • €€€€

8 Strofi
The rooftop view is fantastic, and the food is a cut above the typical taverna fare. The crowd is often filled with theatre types from the nearby Herodes Atticus. ◈ Rovertou Galli 25 • Map B5 • 210 921 4130 • €

9 Edodi
One of Athens' top restaurants, set in an old mansion in Koukaki. The food is superb, unfortunately the space is limited and reservations are essential. (See also p57.) ◈ Veikou 80 • Map C6 • 210 921 3013 • €€€€

10 Psaras
This established, pretty taverna has tables on the white-washed steps leading to the Acropolis. Try the soupes (cuttlefish). ◈ Erectheos 16 & Erotokritiou • Map K4 • 210 321 8733 • €€€

Left **Municipal Art Gallery** Centre **Museum of Traditional Greek Ceramics** Right **Avyssynias Café**

Monastiraki, Psiri, Gazi and Thissio

FOR DECADES THESE OLD NEIGHBOURHOODS *of warehouses and work-shops lay quiet, crumbling and neglected, enlivened only by the Monastiraki flea market, which spills out antiques, kitsch and junk from Plateia Avissynias. However, in recent years the appeal of central location, cheap rent, chic renovated factory space and an authentically funky atmosphere lured first galleries, then clubs, cafés and restaurants, to move into what's now the hippest area in town. Gentrification hasn't robbed these districts of their character, though. Rather, craftsmen's shops and industrial buildings nestle side-by-side with edgy clubs, hole-in-the-wall Greek music dives and squares filled with outdoor cafés and bars. Adding to the mix are views of marble antiquities at the Agora and Kerameikos, Athens' greenest archaeological sites.*

Sights

1 Agora and Agora Museum
2 Technopolis
3 Kerameikos
4 Athens Municipal Art Gallery
5 Athens' Flea Market
6 Plateia Monastiraki
7 Folk Ceramic Museum
8 Hadrian's Library
9 Kapnikarea
10 Athinais

Antiques at Plateia Avyssinias

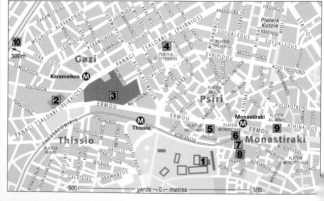

Previous pages **Restaurants in Plaka**

1 Agora and Agora Museum

One of the most interesting archaeological sites in Greece, this is where Socrates "corrupted" youth, St Paul preached and converted his first followers, and the first decisions in the fledgling democracy were made. Don't miss the wonderfully preserved Temple of Hephaestus, or the recreated Stoa of Attalos, now home to the excellent Agora Museum. *(See pp12–15.)*

Stele of Demitria and Pamphile, Kerameikos

2 Technopolis

This enormous complex used to be a toxin-spewing foundry, hence the name of the neighbourhood, "Gazi" (gaslands). These days it's been converted into a huge arts centre, hosting top-notch exhibits, concerts and arts spaces – hence the building's new name, which means "art city". The conversion to Technopolis has prompted a revitalization of the entire area, with trendy bars and restaurants springing up among the gaslands. Check the *Athens News (see p131)* for listings of the frequent events. ◈ *Peiraios 100 • Map A4 • 210 346 7322*

3 Kerameikos

A green oasis in the middle of factories and hardware markets, this is the site of the oldest and largest burial ground in Attica. This is also the outer wall of the ancient city, and running through it is the Sacred Way. Outside the site, the road continues, still incongruously named Sacred Way despite its congested traffic and empty warehouses. *(See pp26–7.)*

4 Athens Municipal Art Gallery

Most important 20th-century Greek artists are represented in this collection of 2,355 works of art. These include paintings and engravings, as well as several drawings by Bavarian architect Ernst Ziller, who designed many of Athens' most important Neo-Classical buildings. Here you can see his plans for the National Theatre and designs for the city's grandest private homes, now mostly converted to museums and public spaces. ◈ *Peiraios 51, Gazi • Map B3 • 9am–1pm & 5–9pm Mon–Fri, 9am–1pm Sun • Free*

Agora

Flea market

5 Athens' Flea Market

Small, seedy Plateia Avissynias comes alive on Sunday mornings when Athens' biggest and most colourful flea market fills the space and spills out to the streets around it. Here's where you'll find everything you didn't know you needed: pink cut-glass Turkish liqueur sets, 100-year-old phones that still work, beautiful antique carved-wood desks, and piles of fantastic kitsch and junk. Bring your haggling skills. ◈ *Plateia Avissynias & Ermou • Map J3*

6 Plateia Monastiraki

There has been a church and monastery on this site since at least the 10th century. The current church was built in 1678. The monastery once owned many of the surrounding buildings, which were later destroyed, but the area's name (Monastiraki means "little monastery") still derives from its glory days. The Pantánassa church, or church of the Dormition of the Virgin, was recently restored, and it reopened in 2007. ◈ *Map J3*

7 Folk Ceramic Museum

This is an outpost of the Museum of Greek Folk Art *(see p70)*, housed in an 18th-century mosque. The museum's extensive collection includes rich, colourful ceramics, beautiful sculpture and decorative folk objects from all over Greece and Asia Minor. Most of the exhibits are made from terracotta or the gleaming faïence that was favoured by the ancient Minoans. ◈ *Areos 1 • Map J3 • 210 324 2066 • 9am–2.30pm daily • Adm*

Figure at the Folk Ceramic Museum

8 Hadrian's Library

Roman Emperor Hadrian built this sumptuous "library" (really more of a luxurious forum) in AD 131. It had a marble courtyard, mosaic floors, concert areas and a small area for storing library scrolls, all surrounded by exquisite Corinthian columns. Following an extensive excavation and restoration project, part of the site is now open to the public. *(See p45.)* ◈ *Map J3 • Summer: 8am–7pm daily; winter: 8am–3pm daily • Adm*

9 Kapnikarea

One of Athens' greatest pleasures is walking down a crowded street and suddenly finding yourself face-to-face with a tiny, centuries-old monument in the midst of all the modern. The beautiful 10th-century church known as Kapnikarea, sma

---

The Jewish Community

The area of Psiri and Kerameikos has been heavily settled by Greek Jews since the third century BC. In 1944, the Nazis occupying Athens sent more than half the population to concentration camps; however, the community has slowly built up to once again become a centre of Greek Jewish life.

Hadrian's Library

the middle of the shopping street of Ermou, provides just such a moment. Built over the ruins of an ancient temple to a goddess, the church kept the theme, with its dedication to the Virgin. ⊗ *Kapnikarea & Ermou • Map K3 • 8am–2pm Mon & Wed, 8am–12:30pm & 5–7pm Tue, Thu, Fri, 8–11:30am Sun • Free*

10 Athinais

A former silk factory converted into a trendy, upmarket arts centre. Athinais has an excellent gourmet restaurant, a stylish bar, a music hall and an old-fashioned cinema. The centre also houses the Museum of Diachronic Art. Check the *Athens News* for events listings. ⊗ *Kastorias 34–36, Votanikos • Map A3 • 210 348 0000 • Museum: open 9am–10pm daily*

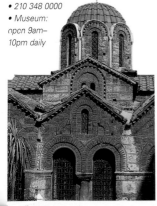

Kapnikarea

Sunday Markets

Morning

🕐 Start the day with the Sunday brunch served in the garden courtyard of the **Athenaeum Maria Callas** *(see p82)*, accompanied by famous opera recordings.

🚫 Satiated with food and music, head for Psirri to the shop of **Stavros Melissinos** *(see p83)*. He will custom-fit you a classic pair of Greek sandals, and possibly try to sell you an English translation of one of his books.

Proceed to Plateia Monastiraki, overlooked by the **Folk Ceramic Museum**. Step inside for a while or take a walk around the closed but visible-to-the-public **Hadrian's Library**.

Early Afternoon

Then head over to the **Roman Agora** *(see pp12–15)*, the sprawling marketplace that was Athens' heart for centuries. Take a good two hours here, making sure not to miss the fantastically well-preserved Temple of Hephaestus and the restored Stoa of Attalos, home to the excellent Agora Museum.

Now that you're warmed up, it's time to go back down Adrianou simply for the fun of haggling at the lively **Flea Market** at Plateia Avissynias. It's hard to resist buying at least something, though by this stage of the day it is more likely to be fabulous kitschy junk than bargain antique.

🚫 Once you're done, retire with your booty to **Café Avissynias** *(p84)* to enjoy a long lunch, as the marketplace closes down and the music and drinking start up.

Left **Flower Market** Right **Plateia Iroon**

Best of the Rest

1 Flower Market
Great bunches of colourful flowers sold around the church of St Irene. A good place to take pictures. ◈ *Plateia Ag Eirinis • Map K3 • Early morning–early afternoon daily*

2 Artio
One of the best-established of the cluster of Psiri galleries, Artio is known for promoting the work of cutting-edge conceptual artists. ◈ *Pallados 3 • Map J2 • noon–4pm & 6–9pm Tue–Fri, noon–4pm Sat*

3 Plateia Iroon
Quintessential Psiri: the square is surrounded by hip bars, old-fashioned tavernas, and dirt-cheap student hangouts. ◈ *Map J2*

4 Cine Psiri
This great outdoor cinema frequently shows black-and-white classics and foreign films (in the original and subtitled in Greek); the *Athens News* has listings. ◈ *Sarri 40–44 • Map B3 • 210 324 7234*

5 First Synagogue of Athens
Before World War II, this area was the centre of Athens' thriving Jewish community. The synagogue is the oldest in Athens. Across the street, Beth-Salom Synagogue is now Athens' main community synagogue. ◈ *Melidoni 8 • Map B4*

6 Athenaeum Maria Callas
This conservatory, named after Greece's native daughter, hosts the annual international Maria Callas Grand Prix opera competition. Sunday breakfast in the courtyard is accompanied by opera records. ◈ *Adrianou 3 • Map B4*

7 Adrianou
The stretch of this street from the Thissio metro to Hadrian's Library offers a wonderful view of the ancient Agora and Acropolis. ◈ *Map K3*

8 Bernier/Eliades Gallery
One of Athens' premiere galleries, Bernier/Eliades exhibits more international artists than any other in Athens, plus top Greek artists. ◈ *Eptachalkou 11 • Map A4*

9 Benaki Islamic Art Museum
In a Neo-Classical town house overlooking Keramikos, four large exhibition rooms display Islamic ceramics, metalwork, wood-carvings, glassware and textiles. ◈ *Agion Asomaton 22 & Dipilou • Map B3 • 210 325 1311 • www.benaki.gr*

10 Irakleidon
Lined with cafés, bars and hipsters, this street feels both old-world and fresh, and bustles day and night. ◈ *Map A4*

Left **Street seller** Centre **Athens' Flea Market** Right **Antiques stalls**

🔟 Bargains, Antiques & Market Stalls

1 Bahar
The whole area around the central meat market teems with old, family-run shops selling traditional foodstuffs. Bahar is one of the best-known for herbs.
⊗ *Evripidou 31 • Map K2*

2 Palaiopoleio Alexandros
You never know what you might unearth among the books, ornaments and moth-eaten clothing piled up in this potential treasure trove. ⊗ *Thisiou 10 • Map B4*

3 Athens' Flea Market
Everything under the sun, from ancient coins to fake designer sunglasses, frilly knickers and antiques at rock-bottom prices *(p80)*.

4 Katerina
This tiny alcove manages to stock a fine selection of traditional wooden *tavli* (backgammon) boards. Prices from as low as €10. ⊗ *Ifaistou 21 • Map J3*

5 Boots & Belts
This shop appears at first to be a wardrobe store for wannabe Hell's Angels. But take in your favourite jeans and the owner, Pantelis, will make you an exact replica in leather for only €300.
⊗ *AG. Theklas 12 (2nd floor) • Map J3*

6 Spiliopoulos
Creations by top shoe designers for as little as half the normal retail price. How can they be so cheap? These shoes are either seconds (usually with no visible flaw) or one-off experimental lines. ⊗ *Adrianou 50 • Map K4*

7 Stavros Melissinos (the Poet Sandalmaker)
This smiling figure opened his shop of lasting, handmade leather sandals in 1954, has expanded the original few styles, and has become a tourist attraction in his own right. ⊗ *AG. Theklas 2 • Map K3*

8 Martinos Antiques
A legend in the Greek antiques market, this three-floor shop gathers furniture, gold and silver, paintings, carpets, books and ornaments from all over the world. ⊗ *Pandrosou 50 • Map K3*

9 Aristokratikon
Using only the finest Greek ingredients, freshly handmade every day, these chocolates are strictly for connoisseurs.
⊗ *Karageorgi Servias 9*

10 Kalyviotis
Thread and fabric, bead- and button-filled shops populate the area around Ermou and Perikleous. Kalyviotis is the best one-stop haberdashery. ⊗ *Ermou 8 • Map L3*

Left **Pil Poule** Right **Café Avissynias**

Café Aeolis
1 Ladies who lunch and writer-types fill this bright, trendy café for light lunches and, later, the tables outside for wine and cocktails. ⊗ *Aiolou 23 • Map K3 • €*

Thanassis
2 Athens' most famous *souvlaki* joint has been serving up hot, juicy, thinly sliced beef, slathered with cool garlicky tzatziki, wrapped in tender pittas, since the 19th century. ⊗ *Mitropoleos 69 • Map K3 • €*

Café Avissynias
3 While away Sunday after-noons overlooking the Mona-stiraki market in this hidden *belle époque* gem. French and Arab food and music. ⊗ *Plateia Avissynias • Map J3 • Closed Mon • €*

Oineas
4 Fun, high-quality, modern taverna-food-with-a-twist. Share one massive salad among five, then pass around bite-sized *spana-kopitas* (spinach pies) and balsamic chicken. ⊗ *Aisopou 9 • Map J2 • €*

To Varoulko
5 The menu at Athens' top fish restaurant changes daily depending on what the sea brings forth. Sleek modern wood-and-glass interior. ⊗ *Pireos 80 • Map B3 • 210 522 8400 • Closed Sun • €€€€*

Pil Poule
6 From the red-carpeted entrance to the lovely marble roof garden (with a gorgeous view), the fine surroundings match the exquisite Franco-Mediterranean cuisine. *(See p57.)* ⊗ *Apostolou Pavlou 51 • Map B4/5 • 210 345 0803 • €€€€€*

Kitrino Podilato
7 Serves innovative food in style. Try the smoked salmon with whisky. Plous Podilato is a sister restaurant in Piraeus *(see p106).* ⊗ *Kerameikou 114–116 • Map A3 • 210 346 5830 • €€€€*

Hytra
8 Mediterranean cuisine in a minimalist dining space brought to hip Psiri by the owners of Spondi *(see p56).* ⊗ *Navarhou Apostoli 7 • Map B4 • 210 331 6767 • €€€*

Mamacas
9 Taverna food made stylish, but with a deep respect for its most important element: bright, fresh flavour. *(See p57).* ⊗ *Persephonis 41, Gazi • €€*

To Kouti
10 Informal and fun, To Kouti offers Greek dishes with a creative twist, and a perfect view of the Acropolis from its outdoor tables. ⊗ *Adrianou 23, Monastiraki • Map B4 • 210 321 3229 • €€*

→ **Note:** Unless otherwise stated, all restaurants accept credit cards and serve vegetarian meals

Left **Cubanita** Right **Spirit Bar**

🔟 Nightspots

Hoxton
Located opposite the new Kerameikos metro station, in a former warehouse, this hip industrial-style lounge stages art and photography exhibitions.
◈ Voutadon 42, Gazi • Map A4

Nipiagogio
This former kindergarten (as its Greek name suggests) has been turned into a friendly little club, with a great atmosphere. In the summer dancing moves outside to the courtyard garden.
◈ Elasidon & Kleanthous 8, Gazi • Map A3

Gazaki
An easy-going, arty crowd enjoy good conversation and music in this late-night bar.
◈ Triptopolemou 31, Gazi

Spirit Bar
A mixed crowd packs this two-storey club, dominated by a huge gold-beaded chandelier. There's cosy seating and plenty of room for dancing to funk and trip-hop. ◈ Miaouli 13 • Map J2/3

Cubanita
Serious Spanish and South American dancers dominate the dancefloor nightly; if you're not up to the challenge, just enjoy the great Cuban food and music.
◈ Karaiskaki 28 • Map J2/3

Thirio
In this old house turned bar, ll stone rooms seem to follow essly from one to another,

dimly lit by star-shaped lights and candles. Sink in and enjoy the jazz. ◈ Lepeniotou 1 • Map B4

Fidelio
Pink and white swags from the ceiling, candles dripping on old silver candelabras, antique furniture and Athens' hipsters of all ages relaxing. ◈ Ogygou 2 & Apostoli • Map B4

Bios
With a ground level bar and a basement club, Bios stages alternative theatre and concerts, with an emphasis on electronica. Popular with art and design students. ◈ Peiraios 84, Gazi • Map B3

Soul
Stylish but fun and informal. It has a stunning courtyard garden with Chinese lanterns, deep red walls and lush planting.
◈ Evripidou 65 • Map B3

Bartessera
Combining a bar, an airy internal courtyard and a small exhibition space, Bartessera is open all day but really livens up at night. ◈ Kolokotroni 4, Monastiraki • Map K3

Around Athens – Monastiraki, Psiri, Gazi and Thissio

Recommend your favourite bar on traveldk.com

85

Left **Plateia Exarcheia** Centre **Cultural Centre of Athens** Right **Strefi Hill**

Omonia and Exarcheia

EXARCHEIA AND OMONIA are among Athens' oldest, most well-worn districts. Though neither qualifies as beautiful, both are steeped in history, some of it quite recent. In 1973, the Polytechnic student uprising in Exarcheia was crushed by the junta, but it did eventually lead to the fall of the hated military dictatorship. The students left behind a neighbourhood full of cafés alive with political debate; this is also the best place to hear rembetika, the gritty Greek blues. Below Exarcheia is seedy, clamorous Omonia, and just beyond is the colourful marketplace district.

Left **National Archaeological Museum** Right **Academy of Arts**

🔟 Sights

1. Central Market
2. Plateia Klafthmonos
3. City of Athens Museum
4. Athens University and Academy of Arts
5. Plateia Omonia
6. Plateia Exarcheia
7. Polytechnic
8. Epigraphical Museum
9. National Archaeological Museum
10. Pediou tou Areos

Central Market

Central Market
The enormous meat, fish and spice markets are a sensory overload, especially the first, but shouldn't be missed by any but the most squeamish. Several restaurants and even a rembetatiko dot the meat market, serving up the sales of the day until dawn. Outside, the air around the spice stores, centred on Athinas, is redolent with vanilla, saffron and dried mountain thyme. ◈ *Map K1/2 • 7am–3pm Mon–Sat*

Plateia Klafthmonos
This square has long played a role in Athens' political history. Its name comes from the ancient Greek word for "crying", which is applied here because of the tradition of politicians commiserating at this square if they have suffered election losses. It is also a site of rallies, demonstrations and concerts. ◈ *Map L2*

City of Athens Museum
This was the first house built in Athens after it was declared capital of the new kingdom of Greece in 1834. Otto, Greece's first king, had it joined with next door, and lived here while he waited for the first Royal Palace (now Parliament) to be built. Today the old residence houses a collection of paintings and furnishings telling the modern city's history, with a focus on the War of Independence *(see p34)* and the first years of the monarchy. ◈ *Paparrigopoulou 7 • Map L2 • 210 324 6164 • 9am–4pm Mon, Wed & Fri, 10am–3pm Sat • Adm*

Athens University and Academy of Arts
The city's university, Academy of Arts and National Library *(see p90)* make up a trio of the most important Neo-Classical buildings in Athens. The column bases and capitals of the university entrance are replicas of those in the Acropolis Propylaia, and the Academy entrance draws from the eastern side of the Erechtheion. The university's frescoes depict personifications of the arts around the modern king, Otto. ◈ *Panepistimiou • Map L/M1–2*

City of Athens Museum

Academy of Arts

Plateia Omonia
5 One hundred years ago, Omonia was among the largest, most gracious and important central squares in Athens. These days, while still large and central, it is also the hang-out spot for prostitutes, porn peddlers, drug addicts, street hawkers and bewildered tourists, as well as a constant chaotic tangle of traffic and construction. Having said all that, in preparation for the 2004 Olympics, Omonia underwent a major renovation, with art installations brought in, a pedestrian walkway created and a scheme to restore its once-beautiful Neo-Classical façades. ✎ Map C2

Plateia Exarcheia
6 It may seem a little worn around the edges, but this is the place to be for all your liberal intellectual café-sitting needs. The roads leading up to it are covered with graffiti decrying the latest actions of Western imperialist governments, and blanketed with leaflets advertising the latest demonstration of the

17 November 1973
The 1973 students of the Polytechnic are the great heroes of the modern Greek state. On 17 November 1973, they demonstrated against the junta, which had been in power since 1967. The uprising was crushed with tanks and guns. But their courage eventually led to the junta's fall and the country's liberation the following year.

week. De rigueur frappé-sipping attire is unruly hair, black turtlenecks and messenger bags. Of course, there is also a jaded awareness of Exarcheia's reputation – as seen at the likes of the cutesy creperie called "Anarchy". At night it's an atmospheric place to be as the rembetika music starts up. ✎ Map D2

Polytechnic
7 This is where the student demonstrations in 1973 *(see box)* began. And in front of the Polytechnic there is a marble statue of a youth lying on the ground – a monument to the fallen heroes of the uprising. Every year on 17 November, all of Greece's politicians turn out to put flowers at the memorial. ✎ Map C/D1

Epigraphical Museum
8 Housed here is one of the world's most precious collections of ancient inscriptions, including the official records of early

Fallen Student at the Polytechnic

Athens, carved on stone and marble slabs. It's a fascinating trove of Athenean lore, and the most important exhibits include: a decree by the assembly of Athens ordering the evacuation of the city before the Persian invasion in 480 BC; a sacred law concerning temple-worship on the Acropolis; and a stele carved with accounts of the construction of the Erechtheion at the Acropolis some 2,400 years ago.
⊗ Tositsa 1 • Map D1 • 210 821 7637 • 8:30 am–3pm Tue–Sun • Free

National Archaeological Museum

This almost peerless collection is the mother lode of archaeological displays in a country that could arguably claim to be the mother lode of important archaeological sites. Highlights include the golden hoard of Homer's Mycenae and the great Classical marble sculptures, plus everything in between. (See also pp16–17 and 46.)

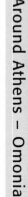

Dipylon Amphora, Archaeological Museum

Pediou tou Areos

The largest park in Athens is green and spacious, although not as densely planted and lovely as the National Gardens. Despite its size, Pediou tou Areos has more of a feel of a neighbourhood park, with old ladies sitting on benches and kids riding bikes. Because of its close proximity to political and intellectual Exarcheia, it is often the scene of rallies, outdoor concerts and cultural events such as the annual book fair. (See also p53.) ⊗ Leoforos Alexandras • Map D1

A Day Around Omonia

Morning

Start at Greece's greatest treasure storehouse: the **National Archaeological Museum**. Spend around 90 minutes, making sure to see the Mycenean Treasure, Thira Frescoes and Classical statuary.

When leaving the museum, turn left on Patission, noting the neighbouring **Polytechnic**, scene of 1973's historic protests. Outside the building, a marble figure lies on the ground, memorializing the fallen students.

Turn left on Stournari, and head for **Plateia Exarcheia** for a frappé and to watch the punks, anarchists and models go by. In summer, head to **Yiantes** (p92) for an alfresco lunch.

Afternoon

Venture downhill on Themistokleous, where most of Greece's independent filmmakers have their offices. Go through Plateia Omonia, just to see Athens' most chaotic spot, but get out as quickly as possible, on Athinas.

You'll pass **Athens City Hall** (see p90) on your right before turning left on Sophocleous. Go down this street to see the **National Bank of Greece**, built on stilts over part of the Themistoklean Wall.

Double back to get to the city's real heart – **Central Food Market** (see p87). Lose yourself in the sights, sounds and smells of the stalls. If it's not summer, finish up at **Stoa Athanaton** (see p93), the city's best rembetatiko, for fantastic music and a delicious traditional meal.

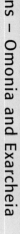

Around Athens – Omonia and Exarcheia

Left **National Theatre** Right **Athens City Hall**

🔟 Best of the Rest

1 National Theatre
The majestic outlines of Hadrian's Library served as the model for this fine Neo-Classical building's façade. Performances by the National Theatre troupe are Greece's finest. ◈ *Agiou Konstantinou 22 • Map B2 • 210 522 3242*

2 Athens City Hall
The headquarters for managing Athens' chaotic sprawl. The archaeological dig in front reveals an area just outside Athens' old city walls. ◈ *Athinas 63 • Map J1*

3 Rebecca Camhi Gallery
This gallery presents both Greek and foreign contemporary artists. Visits by appointment. Check the website for current exhibitions. ◈ *Themistokleous 80 (3rd floor) • Map D2 • www.rebeccacamhi.com*

4 Agioi Theodoroi
A tiny, peaceful 11th-century church in the bustle of the marketplace. The wall paintings are 19th century. ◈ *Plateia Agion Theodoron • Map K2*

5 National Library
One of the important Neo-Classical trio of downtown buildings (see p87). Venture in to admire the library's gorgeous reading room. ◈ *Panepistimiou 28–29 • Map L1 • 9am–2pm Mon–Fri*

6 National Opera
The acoustics aren't great and the Megaron Moussikis draws far more international stars, but the loyal generations who come in furs and lacquered hairdos will always feel at home here. ◈ *Akadimias 59–61 • Map L1*

7 Cultural Centre of Athens
Free exhibits by contemporary Greek artists, a theatre museum, and a lovely café with great people-watching potential. ◈ *Akadimias 50 • Map M1 • 210 362 1601 • 9am–1pm, 5pm–9pm Tue–Sat*

8 Agios Nikolaos Pefkakia
Built in 1895, the church of Agios Nikolaos Pefkakia (St Nicholas of the Pines) crowns the top of steep Dervenion, and is a looming landmark on all the streets below. ◈ *Asklipiou • Map E2*

9 Odos Kallidromiou
Come to the colourful Saturday street market here for a real feeling of the vibrant community of Exarcheia. ◈ *Map D2*

10 Strefi Hill
It's not the prettiest – or cleanest – hill in Athens, but it does give a great view over the whole of the gritty, soulful neighbourhoods of Exarcheia and Omonia. ◈ *Anexartisias and Emmanouil Benaki • Map E1*

Left **Eleftheroudakis** Centre **Karavan** Right **Zolotas**

🔟 Places to Shop

1 Loumidis
This vast corner coffee shop specializes in the traditional Greek/ Turkish brew, selling a selection of *brikia* in which to boil it, cups and saucers, and sweet treats. ⌖ *Aiolou 106 • Map C2*

2 Notos Galleries
One of the few department stores in this country of small shops and boutiques, with an impressive range of local and international goods. ⌖ *Aiolou 99 • Map C3*

3 Stoa tou Vivliou
In the midst of the bustling commercial heart of Athens, this tranquil, recently renovated arcade gathers together a wealth of book-shops, binders and antiquarian outlets. ⌖ *Between Panepistimiou, Pezmazoglou & Stadiou • Map C3*

4 Nakas Musical Instruments
Five floors of everything a musi-cian could need or desire, from traditional painted bouzoukia to fragile violins, sheet music, DJ decks, mixers and very loud speakers. ⌖ *Navarinou 13 & Mavromichali • Map D2/3*

5 Tsitouras
Lavish, extra-vagant and beautiful household objects, wedding and chris-tening gifts, bed-sheets and towels, crockery and cutlery. ⌖ *Solonos 80 • Map D3*

6 Eleftheroudakis
Seven storeys of English and Greek books, with an entire floor devoted to travel, plus the Platis café serving delicious carrot cake, make this the perfect book store. ⌖ *Panepistimiou 17 • Map M2*

7 Zolotas
Celebrated for its intricate creations in hammered gold, Zolotas jewellery has long been one of Athens' most treasured brands. ⌖ *Panepistimiou 10 • Map M2*

8 Karavan
Choose from the scrumptious baklava and kataifi at this tiny but deservedly popular alcove of a shop. ⌖ *Voukourestiou 11 • Map M2*

9 Zoumboulakis Gallery
This celebrated art gallery and shop has a spectacular selection of original paintings and signed, numbered prints by many of Greece's finest artists. ⌖ *Kriezotou 7 • Map M3*

10 Athens Design Centre
Bold, bright bowls, platters, vases and ornaments, some decorated with stripes, zigzags and naïve painted fruit, others just left plain and natural. ⌖ *Valaritou 4 • Map M2*

Left **Barba Yannis** Centre **Kafeneion to Naufayio ton Aggelon** Right **Athinaikon**

Ouzeries and Mezedopoleia

1 Efemero
Two cats wind around wooden benches in this old Athens house waiting for generous patrons to toss them scraps of the excellent pork roasted with peppercorns and olives. ◈ *Themistokleous & Methonis • Map D2 • €*

2 Barba Yannis
There's no sign, but you'll spot this cult favourite by all the students tucking into Uncle John's hearty dirt-cheap dishes. ◈ *Emmanouil Benaki 94 • Map D2 • €*

3 Cookou Food
Taverna dishes with a twist and a pinch of spice are served in this funky, gay-friendly eatery. ◈ *Themistokleous 66 • Map D2 • 210 383 1955 • €*

4 Yiantes
Creative taverna classics – chicken with honey, raisins and coriander – served in a beautiful courtyard. Most of the produce is organic. ◈ *Valtetsiou 44 • Map D2 • 210 330 1369 • €*

5 Taverna Rozalia
Hipsters and locals flock to this pleasant, family-owned mezedopoleion. It has a cosy, wood-beamed interior that's ideal for winter and a courtyard for lazy summer nights. ◈ *Valtetsiou 58 • Map D2 • 210 330 2933 • €*

6 Kafeneion to Naufayio ton Aggelon
Original floor tiles still pave these two tiny rooms, the Angel's Shipwreck. Duck downstairs for octopus and garlicky beetroot with your ouzo. ◈ *Stournari 41 • Map C2 • 210 380 7061 • €*

7 Athinaikon
A beloved central Athens institution, especially among journalists, who trade stories at the marble-topped tables. The plentiful mezes are consistently good. ◈ *Themistokleous 2 • Map C2 • 210 383 8485 • €*

8 Meat Market Restaurant
Everything's made from the market wares of the day, and it's open 'til dawn. Clubbers head here after long nights. ◈ *Map J1 • €*

9 Skoufias
Opened in 2006, Skoufias was an instant hit with the locals due to the colourful interior, tasty Cretan cuisine and low prices. ◈ *Lontou 4, Exarcheia • Map D2 • 210 382 8206 • €*

10 Klimataria
In a grey, seedy part of Omonia stands this warm, old-world taverna. The floors are painted red, the wine barrels decorated with vibrant flowers. ◈ *Plateia Theatrou 2 • Map J1 • 210 321 6629 • €*

Note: *In Ouzeries and Mezedopoleia it is customary to pay in cash; vegetarian dishes are plentiful. For price categories see p101*

Left **Stoa Athanaton** Right **Rembetiki Istoria**

🔟 Rembetatika and Rock Clubs

1 Stoa Athanaton
Athens' premiere rembeta-tiko, open day and night. Old-timers with cigars shower musicians with flowers, and, when the mood strikes, dance to gritty songs of heartbreak. Reserve on Friday and Saturday. ◊ *Central market (in arcade)* • *Map J1*

2 Underworld
This dark club plays rock, industrial and gothic music, and stages fetish performances by international artists. ◊ *Themistokleous & Gamvetta 5* • *Map C2*

3 Lab 22
Offering concerts and theme evenings, such as the ever-popular "kitscharella", this venue is part of the long-standing Club 22 group, known for reinventing itself each year. ◊ *Kiafas 13 (off Zoodochou Pigis & Akadimias)* • *Map D2*

4 An
One of Athens' oldest and best-loved live music clubs, showcasing rock and alternative bands. Rave parties after 1am ◊ *Solomou 13–15* • *Map C2*

5 Taximi
Most of Greece's greatest rembetatika musicians have played here, and the atmosphere retains something of a bygone age. ◊ *Charilau Trikoupi & Isavron 29* • *Map E2*

6 Decadence (Rock Alternative)
Greek alternative music kids and hipsters flock here to dance to the likes of Scotland's Belle & Sebastian and Australia's prince of darkness, Nick Cave. ◊ *Voulgaroktonou 69 & Poulcherias 2* • *Map E1*

7 Mo Better
Fun and chaotic, this dark little rock club plays old favourites such as the Violent Femmes, often staying open till sunrise. ◊ *Themistokleous & Koletti 32* • *Map D2*

8 Rembetiki Istoria
The original moulded walls and ceilings of this favourite bar, tucked into an early 20th-century building, are a nice contrast with the earthy music. ◊ *Ippokratous 181* • *Map E2*

9 Parafono
A great little jazz and blues cabaret that for 25 years has attracted some of the best names in the business to its small stage, draped with plush red curtains. ◊ *S Kinnis 1 & Asklipeiou 130* • *Map F2*

10 Kavouras
A dark and smoky rembetatiko den upstairs: all-night souvlaki joint under the same name can be found on the ground floor. ◊ *Themistokleous 64* • *Map D2*

Rembetatika are clubs specializing in rembetika, often dubbed the "Greek blues"

Left **Kallimarmaro Stadium** Centre **Plateia Syntagma** Right **Benaki Museum**

Syntagma and Kolonaki

PLATEIA SYNTAGMA IS THE CENTRE OF MODERN ATHENS, crowned by the large, Neo-Classical Parliament building. Standing sentry outside are the evzones – soldiers marching solemnly back and forth in traditional short skirts and pompommed shoes. By Parliament, on the wide, tree-lined avenue of Vasilissis Sofias is Museum Row: many of Athens' finest museums are here. Behind Syntagma is posh Kolonaki, home to ambassadors, models, movie stars and the fabulous designer boutiques that cater to them. This is the prime spot for shopping, people-watching and glamorous but pricey café-sitting. **Evzone soldier** Rising above it all is Lykavittos Hill, topped by a famous outdoor theatre, and gorgeous cafés and restaurants with a view to die for.

Sights

1. Kallimarmaro Stadium
2. National Gardens
3. National Parliament Building
4. Syntagma Metro Station
5. Evzones
6. Benaki Museum
7. Museum of Cycladic Art
8. Byzantine Museum
9. War Museum
10. Lykavittos Hill

Museum of Cycladic Art

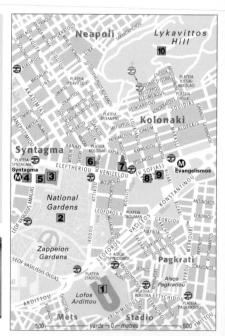

1 Kallimarmaro Stadium

The formal name of this stadium is the Panathenaic, but it's more commonly known as Kallimarmaro, meaning "beautiful marble". Built in 330 BC for the Panathenaic games, it later fell into disuse. In 1895, George Averoff had it restored with fine Pentelic marble, and it hosted the first modern Olympics in 1896. In 2004, it provided the final circuit for the Olympic Marathon and also hosted the archery competition. *(See p62.)* Ⓢ *Vas Konstantinou • Map N6 • 8:30am–1pm & 3:30pm–7pm Mon–Fri*

2 National Gardens

The huge, shady National Gardens are an unexpected green refuge in parched central Athens. They were originally planted in 1839 as the Royal Garden of Queen Amalia, who had her horticulturalists bring in 15,000 domestic and exotic plants, many of which remain. The garden was opened to the public in 1923. Many statues dot the garden. It also has a small zoo, a duck pond and a playground. *(See p52.)* Ⓢ *Amalias • Map M4*

3 National Parliament Building

The imposing building was constructed in 1842 as a palace

National Gardens

for Otto, Greece's first king after independence. Over the next 70 years, it suffered neglect and in 1923, during a housing shortage, it acted as a homeless shelter. After the return of parliamentary government in 1926, the building was gutted, renovated and re-opened as a single-chamber council for parliament. Today it is the scene of debates that range from the hilariously surreal to the stultifyingly boring, viewable on state television via a live video link. Its library can be visited. Ⓢ *Plateia Syntagma • Map M3 • Library: 9am–1:30pm Mon–Fri*

4 Syntagma Metro Station

Syntagma station is as much museum as transport hub. When the city was busy excavating to extend the metro, archaeologists found thousands of priceless items on this site, which has been continuously occupied since Classical times. Many are displayed in the station, but the highlight is a glass wall overlooking the site, which includes at least two cemeteries. *(See p44.)* Ⓢ *Map M3*

National Parliament Building

Evzones

5 On guard in front of Parliament are the famous *evzones*, soldiers in the traditional attire of the rebels who won the War of Independence. It's hard to imagine fighting efficiently in this uniform: a short white skirt (with 400 pleats, symbolizing the years under Turkish rule), red cap, and red pompommed shoes. The changing of the guard is like a slow high-kick dance. *Evzones* are selected from the tallest and handsomest men in the mandatory Greek military service. ◉ *Map M3 • Changing of the guard every hour*

Benaki Museum

6 The Benaki is one of Greece's pre-eminent museums, not only for its extensive and top-notch collection of prehistoric to 20th-century Greek art, but also because it's a lovely place to be. Among its highlights are the re-creations of Ottoman-style sitting rooms in 18th-century northern Greek mansions, and sumptuous Byzantine shrines. The superb books and jewellery in the gift shop and the rooftop garden restaurant are destinations in themselves. *(See pp22–3 and 47.)*

Byzantine Museum

Ziller the Thriller

When German King Otto was established as the first monarch after independence, he brought with him architect Ernst Ziller to rebuild the city. Ziller's pumped-up Neo-Classicism can be seen in buildings such as the Cycladic Museum, the Numismatic Museum *(p98)* and King Constantine's Palace – today, the official Presidential mansion *(p98)*.

Museum of Cycladic Art

7 Some 2,000 years before the Parthenon, a mysterious civilization on the Cycladic islands created the prototypical Mediterranean marble sculptures: simple, elemental female forms. The figures still resonate today, famously influencing artists like Modigliani and Picasso. The Goulandris family, one of Greece's oldest shipping and philanthropic dynasties, displays the world's largest collection of Cycladic art in a beautifully restored Neo-Classical mansion. There are often exhibits by top contemporary Greek and international artists in the extra-swanky new wing. *(See pp18–19 and 47.)*

Byzantine Museum

8 The museum's 15,000 objects (only a fraction of which are displayed at any one time) date from the 3rd to the 19th century, chronicling the rise and decline of the great Byzantine Empire. There are priceless sculptures, icons and richly worked gold and silver religious trappings. The permanent collection is housed in a smart new two-level space built partially underground, which opened in summer 2004. *(See pp28–9 and 47.)*

War Museum

9 The two huge floors telling the history of warfare in Greece from prehistoric to modern times might not be everyone's cup of tea, but most will enjoy the Saroglos collection, including medieval suits of armour, three-musketeer-type duelling foils,

War Museum

and fabulous engraved Turkish scimitars. Outside, there are several fighter planes and tanks – visitors are allowed to climb up and take a look in the cockpits of most of them. *(See p47.)* ◈ *Vas Sofias • Map E/F4 • 9am–2pm Tue–Sun • Free*

Lykavittos Hill

[10] Steep Lykavittos Hill juts high out of Kolonaki, and the church at its peak is visible for miles around. Every summer, the Lykavittos Festival hosts a variety of top musicians from around the world in the theatre close to the church; there's nothing like watching Bob Dylan or Guru with the sun going down over Athens behind them *(see p61)*. A smart café-restaurant nestles below the church. If you are very, very ambitious, walk up – otherwise, take the funicular from Aristipou. ◈ *Map F2*

Lykavittos Hill

An Afternoon in Chic Kolonaki

Mid-Afternoon

🕐 Start at **Plateia Syntagma** a few minutes before the hour to see the changing of the guard in front of the Tomb of the Unknown Soldier. Then head up Vasilissis Sofias to the **Museum of Cycladic Art** to ponder the mysterious prehistoric marble sculptures. Be sure to check out whatever temporary exhibition is on at the adjoining Stathatos Mansion – they are usually small but world-class shows.

Then it's on to **Plateia Kolonaki** for a frappé and a pastry at one of the roadside cafés and some stellar people-watching. The parade of wealthy wives, pretty playboys and Greek starlets provides recompense for overpriced drinks – just sip slowly!

Late Afternoon

Afterwards, fan out from the square for some serious shopping or browsing of the shop windows and eyeing patrons at **Folli Follie, Prasini** and **Elena Votsi** *(see p99)*, as well as familiar international stables such as Gucci, Armani and Versace.

Towards the end of the day, go to the funicular station at the foot of **Lykavittos Hill**. Though close to Plateia Kolonaki, the walk is quite steep, so if you're feet are tired you can take the 060 minibus from the square or a two-minute taxi ride. From the hilltop at dusk, watch the sky turn violet over Athens, while enjoying a drink at the café, or a truly special meal at **Orizontes** restaurant *(see p101)*.

Left **Tomb of the Unkown Soldier** Right **Plateia Kolonaki**

🔟 Best of the Rest

1 Zappeion
The 19th-century Zappeion stands in pleasant grounds at the southern end of the National Gardens. Its tree-lined paths are open to the public, while the Zappeion itself hosts international conferences. ◈ Map M5

2 Presidential Palace and Maximou Mansion
The former palace of King Constantine was designed by Ernst Ziller (p96). Next door, Maximou is the Prime Minister's official residence – though present incumbent Costas Simitis prefers his Kolonaki apartment. ◈ Corner of Irodou Attikou and Vasileos Georgiou • Map N4

3 Tomb of the Unknown Soldier
A dying soldier, carved in 1930 on the wall in front of the Parliament, commemorates Greece's war dead since the War of Independence (p34). ◈ Plateia Syntagma • Map M3

4 National Historical Museum
Greece's first parliament building, this is now a museum specializing in the War of Independence. ◈ Stadiou 13, Plateia Kolokotroni • Map L2 • 9am–2pm Tue–Sun • Adm

5 Numismatic Museum/ Schliemann's House
This collection of coinage is housed in the mansion of Heinrich Schliemann, discoverer of the Mycenae treasure. ◈ Panepistimiou 12 • Map M2 • 8:30am–3pm Tue–Sun • Adm

6 Museum of the History of Greek Costume
Over 6,000 items of clothing, jewellery and adornments showing the variety of Greek dress through the ages. ◈ Dimokritou 7 • Map M2 • 10am–1:30pm Mon–Fri • Free

7 Plateia Kolonaki
The hottest spot for people-watching in trendy Kolonaki. Enjoy overpriced drinks and watch the beautiful people go by. ◈ Map N3

8 Plateia Dexameni
Greener and lower-key than Plateia Kolonaki, and home to one of Athens' nicest outdoor cinemas. ◈ Map N/P2

9 Friday Morning Street Market
One of Athens' most vital fruit 'n' veg markets. ◈ Xenokratous • Map P2

10 Gennadius Library
This library of multilingual volumes is among the world's best for all subjects Hellenistic. ◈ Souidias 61 • Map F3 • 9am–5pm Mon–Wed & Fri, 9am–8pm Thu, 9am–2pm Sat

Left **Elena Votsi** Centre **Folli Follie** Right **Prasini** shoe shop

⏉10 Chic Boutiques

1 Folli Follie
Attractive, high-quality and affordably priced watches, neck-laces, bracelets, bags and other accessories. ◈ *Solonos 25 • Map N2*

2 Antonios Markos
As well as his quirky own-label tailoring, Markos imports an eclectic mix of items from both world-famous and lesser-known brands. ◈ *Skoufa 21 • Map N2*

3 Amelie
Concept cake shopping. This exceptionally chic patissier sells delectable pastel-hued macaroons, chocolates and desserts. ◈ *Pinda-rou 29 & Anagnostopoulou • Map N2*

4 Yeshop
Edgy, directional pieces from one of Greece's brightest young design stars. Yiorgos Eleftheriades specializes in distressed tailoring and unique designs for fashion-able guys and girls. ◈ *Pindarou 38 • Map N2*

5 Bettina
Bettina's impressive stock includes international labels alongside Greece's own Angelos Frentzos and Sophia Kokosalaki. ◈ *Pindarou 40 • Map N2*

6 Optika Arathymos
Check out a wide selection of the latest and trendiest designer shades at this small, well-stocked shop, where the staff are knowledgeable and the prices reasonable. ◈ *Kanari 10 • Map N3*

7 Prasini
Offering some of the very best in Greek, Spanish and Italian shoe design, Prasini is a hot favourite for wistful window shoppers and Athens' many credit-card-wielding shoe-aholics. ◈ *Tsakalof 7–9 • Map N2*

8 Elena Votsi
One of the up-and-coming names on the international jewellery circuit, Votsi's chunky, rough-edged investment pieces are worth every penny of their pricey tags. ◈ *Xanthou 7 • Map N/P2*

9 Kalogirou
Stocks an overwhelming array of designer shoes and a wide selection of Kalogirou's own stylish creations. ◈ *Patriarchou Ioakeim 4 • Map P2*

10 Lena Katsanidou – Where to Wear
Lena Katsanidou's Kolonaki bou-tique and upstairs atelier sells highly desirable items including her signature line of bold, heavy-weight earrings fashioned in silver and bronze. ◈ *Alopekis 17 & Loukianou • Map P2/3*

Left **Mommy** Centre **Jackson Hall** Right **Rock'n'Roll**

TOP 10 Hot Nightspots

1 Mommy
This small, diverse bar and restaurant takes over the neighbouring pavements at weekends as patrons spill out, drinks in hand. ⊗ *Delfon 4 • Map M1 • 210 361 9682*

2 Skoufaki
Small, dimly lit, smoky and full of artists and actor types, Skoufaki is Kolonaki's most famous, longest-established alternative café and bar. ⊗ *Skoufa 47–49 • Map M1*

3 Jackson Hall
This all-American diner serves beer and burgers with fries among film-star memorabilia. But, this being Kolonaki, Fashion TV plays on large screens and the waitresses are skimpy model-types. ⊗ *Milioni 4 • Map N2*

4 Central
The hottest drinking and socializing spot in town. Packed from mid-afternoon onwards at the weekends, when the beautiful people drop in. ⊗ *Plateia Kolonaki 14 • Map N3 • 210 724 5938*

5 Sea Satin
Drink and eat the chic Greek way at this atmospheric fish taverna and bar where designer-clad 30-somethings dance on the tables to bouzouki-with-a-beat hits. ⊗ *Fokilidou 1 • Map N2 • 210 361 9646*

6 Frame
Ultra-cool lounge bar and restaurant. The all-white summer garden is set in a peaceful park; across the road the indoor area has designer furniture and abstract art. ⊗ *Kleomenous 2 • Map P2*

7 Rock 'n' Roll
There is nothing rock 'n' roll about this Kolonaki classic, just vintage hits, suited businessmen tucking into steak and chips and a Saturday post-shopping crowd. ⊗ *Loukianou & Ipsilantou 6 • Map P3*

8 Briki
Popular with Athenian night owls, Briki is a long-standing little bar which stays open till sunrise, making it the perfect place for a nightcap. ⊗ *Dorilaiou 6, Plateia Mavili*

9 Charitos
Summer or winter, rain or shine, this small pedestrianized section of street lined with tiny bars is always a hive of festivity and conviviality. ⊗ *Map P2*

10 Balthazar
In the gardens of an exquisite Neo-Classical mansion, this elegant bar and restaurant draws an attractive crowd. ⊗ *Tsoha & Soutsou 27 • 210 644 1215*

Left **Kanari Corner** Right **Prytaneio**

Price Categories
For a three-course meal for one with half a bottle of wine (or equivalent meal), taxes and extra charges.

€€€€€ over €60

10 Places to Eat and Drink

1 Orizontes
Enjoy a panoramic view of the capital while feasting on creative Mediterranean and fusion cuisine at the top of Lykavittos Hill. ◈ *Map P1 • 210 722 7065 • €€€€*

2 Kiku
The original and best of the city's now plentiful sushi restaurants. An impeccably presented, tempting selection. ◈ *Dimokritou 12 • Map N2 • 210 364 7033 • €€€€*

3 Altamira
Based in a fine Neo-Classical building, this colourful eatery serves an unusual selection of Mexican, Arabian and Chinese dishes. ◈ *Tsakalof 36a, Kolonaki • Map N2 • 210 361 4695 • €€€*

4 Maritsas
Sit out on the pavement at this traditional, low-profile taverna and enjoy simple and delicious Greek cuisine. Don't miss the delectable *kolokithokeftedes* (courgette fritters). ◈ *Voukourestiou 47 • Map N2 • 210 363 0132 • €€*

5 Kanari Corner
Summer diners in this surprisingly quiet spot tuck into a limited but tasty selection of pastas, salads, grilled meat and desserts. ◈ *Akadimias & Kanari 10 • Map M2 • 210 361 7157 • €€*

6 Prytaneio
Modern Athenian dining at its best. An enticing special is the sea bass with sundried

tomatoes and capers. ◈ *Milioni 7 • Map N2 • 210 364 3353 • €€*

7 Ratka
A Kolonaki classic, this distinguished restaurant is still the preferred dining scene of Athens' elite. Serves a global mix of dishes in refined surroundings. ◈ *Charitos 30 • Map P2 • 210 729 0746 • €€€*

8 To Ouzadiko
Hidden away in an arcade in Kolonaki's heart, this eatery is renowned for its traditional mezes, fresh fish and impressive collection of spirits. ◈ *Karneadou 25–29 • Map P3 • 210 729 5484 • €€*

9 L'Abreuvoir
Traditional French cuisine is offered in style at this established Athenian society haunt. Specializes in meat dishes with extravagant sauces. ◈ *Xenokratous 51 • Map F3 • 210 722 9106 • €€€€*

10 Boschetto
Posh and pricey, this Italian nouvelle cuisine restaurant is prime dining and has an admirable wine list. ◈ *Vasilissis Sofias 46 • Map F4 • 210 721 0893 • €€€€€*

Note: *Unless otherwise stated, all restaurants accept credit cards and serve vegetarian meals*

Left **Bust of Hadrian, Archaeological Museum** Centre **Maritime Museum** Right **Stadium**

Piraeus

RENOWNEDS FOR SEEDY PORTSIDE CAFÉS, *Piraeus is the gateway from Athens to the islands. Abandoned after a glorious ancient birth, it was only redeveloped in 1834. Islanders from Chios, Hydra and Syros set up the first factories, joined by an influx of refugees from Asia Minor in 1922. It soon became the country's main industrial centre, and is now the third-largest Mediterranean port. It underwent a huge makeover for the 2004 Olympics, when giant cruisers served as floating hotels to boost the city's accommodation.*

TOP 10 Sights

1. Pasalimani
2. Hellenic Maritime Museum
3. Akti Themistokleous
4. Archaeological Museum of Piraeus
5. Mikrolimano
6. Yacht Club of Greece
7. Kastella
8. Sunday Morning Flea Market
9. Peace and Friendship Stadium
10. Battleship Averoff

Mikrolimano

Pasalimani cafés

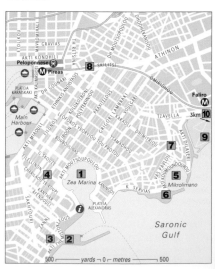

Pasalimani

1 Pasalimani

This large circular bay, with a bottleneck channel opening out to the sea, is surrounded by imposing eight-storey modern apartment blocks. Inaugurated as Athens' main naval base in the 5th century BC, the ancient harbour of Zea could accommodate 196 triremes *(see p40)*. Today, up to 400 of the most impressive motor yachts in Greece moor here. It takes about 20 minutes to walk the perimeter of the bay, along a tree-lined promenade overlooked by open-air cafés.

2 Hellenic Maritime Museum

Housed in a 1960s building by the harbour, this exhibition opens with a map of Odysseus's voyage across the Mediterranean. It then traces the history of Greek naval trading, with models of ships ranging from the 5th-century BC trireme to modern tankers (Greece has the largest merchant fleet in the world). Naval warfare is covered by massive oil paintings of historic sea battles against the Turks, plus flags captured from them.

Grave stele, Archaeological Museum of Piraeus

Ⓢ *Akti Themistokleous, Freatida • 210 428 6959 • 9am–2pm Tue–Fri, 9am–1:30pm Sat • Adm*

3 Akti Themistokleous

From Freatida, a 3-km (2-mile) long lantern-lined coastal promenade, overlooked by modern apartment blocks and a string of informal fish restaurants, offers wonderful views across the open sea to the islands of Aegina and Salamina. The route, named after the 5th-century BC general and statesman Themistoklos, who founded Piraeus, follows the course of the ancient seaward walls. Down below, a series of rocky bays offers the chance of bathing. The prettiest spot of all is Aphrodite's Bay.

4 Archaeological Museum of Piraeus

Standing by the remains of the 2nd-century BC Theatre of Zea, the showpieces here are two Classical bronze statues found in Piraeus in 1959: the proud and perfectly proportioned 5th-century BC Piraeus Apollo and the 4th-century BC Piraeus Athene. Also on display is a collection of 5th- and 4th-century BC marble stele (classical gravestones) with touching reliefs of the deceased. Ⓢ *Odos Charilaou Trikoupi 32 • 210 452 1598 • 8:30am–3pm Tue–Sun • Closed Aug and public hols • Adm*

Left **Mikrolimano** Right **Yacht Club of Greece**

5 Mikrolimano

Best known for its excellent fish restaurants with open-air waterside terraces, this delightful small, circular bay is built on a human scale. The ancients, who kept their ships here, believed it was protected by the goddess Munichia Artemis, and initially named it after her. The Turkish navy used it too, which is why it is still sometimes known as Tourkolimano (Turkish harbour). Today it is filled with the small wooden boats of local fishermen, who supply the surrounding restaurants from their daily catch.

6 Yacht Club of Greece

Europe's top destination for yachters, thanks to its myriad islands, Greece has a 3,500-year tradition of sailing. Set in landscaped gardens on a peninsula on the south side of Mikrolimano, the yacht club was founded in 1934. The main clubhouse is the province of members only, but you can stroll around the marina, then stop for a drink at the chic rooftop café (see p106).
◎ Mikrolimano

7 Kastella

Built into the hillside of Profitis Ilias, which overlooks Mikrolimano, this picturesque residential quarter is filled with pastel-coloured Neo-Classical houses, built between 1834 and 1900, and a labyrinth of steep streets and stairways. There's a village atmosphere here, making it a great area to explore on foot. The highest point is crowned by the church of Profitis Ilias and the Bowling Centre Café (see p107), which offers spectacular views of Athens, while nearby the small open-air Veakeio Theatre is used for staging delightful summer performances.

Lion of Piraeus

During medieval times the main port of Piraeus was known as Porto Leone in tribute to a 3-m (10-ft) tall ancient marble lion, which stood on the site of the present Town Hall. In 1688, the Venetians carried it off and placed it in the Arsenale in Venice. The respective city councils are now negotiating its return.

Kastella

8 Sunday Morning Flea Market

Directly behind Piraeus metro station, in a street parallel to the railway line, this is often compared to Athens' Monastiraki Sunday market (see p80), though it's decidedly grottier. It gets very crowded, attracting tourists, Athenians and local minorities: Albanian immigrants have several shops selling Albanian flags and music, while colourfully dressed gypsies hawk seasonal fruit and nuts. ◈ Omiridou Skilitsi • 8am–2pm Sun

9 Peace and Friendship Stadium

Close to Neo Faliro metro station, this bowl-shaped concrete structure was opened in 1985. Since then it has hosted numerous sporting events, including the 1997 European Basketball Championship, which Greece won, and the 1998 World Basketball Championship. It is also used for rock concerts. At the 2004 Olympics it hosted the volleyball matches. ◈ Off Tzavella Makariou

10 Battleship Averoff

Built in Livorno (Italy) in 1910, this 140-m (460-ft) long battleship was designed to carry 670 men in peacetime and 1,200 during war, and led the Greek fleet through the Balkan Wars and World Wars I and II. Negotiating a series of narrow ladders, you can explore the entire ship, from the kitchen and engine rooms to the main bridge, from the cramped dark space where the crew slept in hammocks, to the contrasting luxury of the officers' mess and the Admiral's sumptuous wooden panelled suite. ◈ Trokantero Marina, Palaio Faliro • 210 983 6539 • 11am–1pm Mon, Wed & Fri, 11am–3pm Sat & Sun • Adm

A Day in Piraeus

Morning/Afternoon

🕐 From Athens, take the metro to Piraeus, then walk to the **Archaeological Museum** (see p103) and check out some of the ancient local finds.

Continue to Pasalimani and stop for a coffee at **Café Freddo** (p107) overlooking the water. Take the time for a stroll around the harbour to admire the top-notch boats.

For a relaxed, indulgent lunch call at **Achinos** (p106), offering fantastic sea views; otherwise walk the seafront promenade of Akti Themistokleous for a reasonably priced informal feast of fresh fish at **Margaro** (p106).

Evening

Take the metro to Neo Faliro, then negotiate a busy main road past the **Peace and Friendship Stadium**, one of Piraeus's beachside venues that was used for the 2004 Olympic Games.

Continue south from the stadium to arrive at the pretty fishing harbour of **Mikrolimano** – less glitzy and more picturesque than the more central bays.

Here you'll find a string of waterside seafood restaurants, the best-known of which is **Jimmy and the Fish** (p106).

After dinner, either escape for a romantic nightcap on the pleasant **Don Kihotis** roof terrace (p107), or join the swelling crowds at **Neon** (p107), one of the café-bars with brash music and open-air seating on Akti Dilaveri.

Price Categories

For a three-course meal for one with half a bottle of wine (or equivalent meal), taxes and extra charges.

€	under €30
€€	€30–€40
€€€	€40–€50
€€€€	€50–€60
€€€€€	over €60

Left **Jimmy & the Fish** Right **Plous Podilatou**

Places to Eat

1 Pisina
Centred on an open-air swimming pool, this modern bar-restaurant is stylish but relaxed. Ⓢ *Marina Zeas, Pasalimani • 210 451 1324 • €€*

2 Dourabeis
Since 1932 Dourabeis has charmed diners with its sublime fresh fish, simply grilled and dressed with lemon and olive oil. Ⓢ *Akti Dilaveri 29, Mikrolimano • 210 412 2092 • €€€*

3 Plous Podilatou
The cool, sleek decor at Plous Podilatou complements an innovative approach to seafood. Ⓢ *Akti Koumoundourou 42, Mikrolimano • 210 413 7910 • €€€*

4 Jimmy & the Fish
Waiters carry platters of smoked tuna and rocket, and pans of lobster to diners on the restaurant's harbourside terrace. Ⓢ *Akti Koumoundourou 46, Mikrolimano • 210 412 4417 • €€€€*

5 Castello
With a lovely rooftop terrace overlooking Microlimano, this bar-restaurant serves up pasta, risotto, salads and a range of delicious meat and fish dishes. The bar stays open till 5am at weekends. Ⓢ *Vas Pavlou 70, Kastella • 210 413 8006*

6 Achinos
Romantic split-level restaurant-bar built into a cliff overlooking the sea. Creative fish, meat and cheese mezes. Ⓢ *Akti Themistokleous 51, Freatida • 210 452 6944 • €€*

7 Diasimos
Two blue-fronted buildings comprise this popular ouzeri and psarotaverna, with lovely views from its seafront terrace. Ⓢ *Akti Themistokleous 306, Freatida • 210 451 4887 • €€*

8 Margaro
A rather limited but heavenly selection of fresh seafood including whitebait, mullet, bream and shrimps. Ⓢ *Chatzikyriakou 126 • 210 451 4226 • Closed Sun dinner and Aug • No credit cards • €*

9 Vassilenas
A set meal of 16 mezes, served up in a steady stream to snack upon. There's a fixed price, and you are advised to book ahead. Ⓢ *Etolikou 72, Agia Sofia • 210 461 2457 • Closed Sun and Aug • No credit cards • €*

10 Kollias
Kollias serves reasonably priced delicious fresh fish, and unusual Greek seafood dishes. It is best reached by taxi as it is not central. Ⓢ *Plastira 3, Tabouria • 210 462 9620 • Closed Sun • €€*

Note: Unless otherwise stated, all restaurants accept credit cards and serve vegetarian meals

Left **Wild Thing** Centre **Iguana** Right **Yacht Club**

TOP10 Bars and Cafés

1 Wild Thing
The first in a row of super-trendy late night café-bars overlooking the Delfinario, Wild Thing pulls in the 30-something crowd. ◎ Akti Dilaveri 16, Mikrolimano

2 Iguana
The young in search of adventure hang out at this bar-nightclub, which plays out disco and techno tracks until 6am – time for an early breakfast. Order water on the terrace if it all gets too much. ◎ Akti Dilaveri 15, Mikrolimano

3 Neon
Open-top jeeps and motorbikes pull up outside this vast bar-nightclub, with white leather armchairs on three levels and industrial air conditioning to keep the atmosphere just right. ◎ Akti Dilaveri 5, Mikrolimano

4 Don Kihotis
A seductive hillside retreat with an old-fashioned interior. Creaky wooden stairs lead to a roof terrace, with dreamy, romantic views. ◎ Vasileos Pavlou 68, Kastella

5 Up Down
Coffee, cocktails and ice creams in a split-level bar with underwater murals and a glass spiral staircase – plus a splendid roof terrace. ◎ Akti Koumoundourou 24, Mikrolimano

6 Love Café
Much hyped bar-restaurant with loud music, young clientele, and 1970s' interior of white plastic furniture with splashes of vibrant red. ◎ Akti Koumoundourou 58, Mikrolimano

7 Istioploikos
One of the hip places to see and be seen, this vast (and packed) rooftop bar commands a vantage point above the yachting marina. ◎ Yacht Club, Mikrolimano
• Open mid-Mar–early Nov

8 Bowling Centre Café
A vast terrace with stunning views from Kastella across the sea to Athens compensates for an impersonal, dated interior. ◎ Profitis Ilias, Kastella

9 Café Freddo
With comfy wicker chairs in a garden overlooking the boats at Pasalimani, stop here for a morning coffee, an afternoon ice cream, a pre-dinner cocktail or a Greek brandy nightcap. ◎ Plateia Alexandras 1, Pasalimani

10 Hard Rock Café
This lofty, wooden-beamed space with leather armchairs and great rock music pulls student backpackers and Greeks who wish they lived elsewhere. ◎ Etolikou 28
• Open to 5am weekends

Left **A Galaxidi café** Centre **Thebes** Right **Osios Loukas**

North to Delphi

THE LANDSCAPE CHANGES *as soon as you drive through Athens' northern suburbs; the sight of pristine, pine-clad Mount Parnitha opens the way to the wide, varied landscape of central Greece. The region, Sterea Ellada, is fringed with mountains, lined with coastal towns and dotted with Byzantine monasteries and ancient ruins. Delphi is the undoubted star and, indeed, the country's most beautiful Classical site. Here, the fabled Oracle voiced its prophecies, telling Oedipus, among others, his terrible fate. Delphi's surrounds are full of beauty and opportunities for swimming, trekking and skiing.*

Delphi's ancient ruins

Sights

1. Dafni
2. Eleusis
3. Mount Parnitha
4. Evia
5. Thebes
6. Osios Loukas
7. Arachova
8. Mount Parnassos
9. Delphi
10. Galaxidi

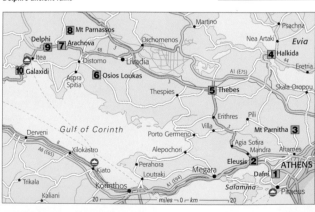

Previous pages Temple of Poseidon, Cape Sounio

Eleusis

1 Dafni

The lovely monastery here is one of the greatest treasures of the Byzantine Empire. Inside, the brilliant mosaics are among the most perfectly executed examples of the genre. It is currently closed for restoration work and is scheduled to reopen in 2008. ◈ Map T2 • 210 581 1558 • Bus A16 to Eleusis from Plateia Eleftherias (30-minute journey to stop at Dafni)

2 Eleusis

For 1,400 years, this was one of Greece's most sacred places. Thousands of pilgrims took part in the Eleusian Mysteries, rites that celebrated Demeter, goddess of nature, and her daughter Persephone. Today Eleusis has become one of Greece's ugliest places – a polluted industrial town. There are still some scattered ruins, though, and a museum to help make sense of them. ◈ Map S2 • 210 554 6019 • Bus A16 as above • 8:30am–3pm Tue–Sun • Adm

3 Mount Parnitha

On the outskirts of Athens, this beautiful mountain has many paths through its dense fir forests, offering walking and trekking for all levels. In spring, its meadows are full of wildflowers. There are two refuges for climbers and a large casino-cum-alpine hotel, reached by cable car from the suburb of Thrakomakedones, and a good starting point for walks. (See also p138.) ◈ Map T2

4 Evia

Greece's second-largest island is so close to the mainland you can reach it by bridge. There are several trains a day from Larissa station in Athens to Chalkida, Evia's central city. The spine of mountains running north to south and dotted with villages offers great weekend trekking, and if you go by car midweek you'll likely have its beaches and the thermal spas at the northern tip to yourself. ◈ Map T1 • Chalkida tourist office: 222 107 7777 • Train times and prices: 210 529 8838

Cloisters, Monastery of Dafni

Oracle of Delphi

The Oracle delivered divine prophecies through a priestess at the Sanctuary of Apollo. The priestess went through consciousness-altering rituals, which probably included chewing laurel leaves and poppies and inhaling the vapours rising from Delphi's natural chasm. She communicated the prophecies in a series of inarticulate cries, which priests translated into verse.

Thebes

The city of Thebes was once one of the greatest Mycenaean settlements and home of the tragic dynasty of Oedipus. Although next to nothing remains of the ancient sites, and the modern city offers little in the way of sightseeing, Thebes is worth a visit for the splendid Archaeological Musuem, with its excellent collection of Mycenaean finds. ✪ Map S2 • Buses hourly from Terminal B • Museum: Apr–Sep: 12–7pm Mon, 8am–7pm Tue–Sun; Oct–Mar: 10:30am–5pm Mon, 8am–3pm Tue–Sun • Adm

Osios Loukas

This is a contender for the most beautiful monastery in Greece, with its idyllic location, looking across a valley to the soaring Elikonas mountain range, and fine Byzantine frescoes within. The interiors of the two distinct 11th-century churches are covered in marvellous mosaic and marble icons and decorations. ✪ Map R1 • 8am–7pm daily (May–Sep: closed 2–4pm) • Adm

Domed ceiling, Osios Loukas

Arachova

This mountain village makes a good alternative base for visiting Delphi and Parnassos. It is an extremely popular winter destination for rich Athenians, and room prices are higher here in winter. Though the main thoroughfare is lined with shops hawking local rugs, honey and cheese, the best way to explore is to get lost in its stone-lined passageways. ✪ Map R1 • Tourist office: 226 703 1630 • Several buses daily from Terminal B, stopping en route to Delphi

Mount Parnassos

Although developed in parts, Mount Parnassos offers fine skiing, splendid views and, in spring, wonderful trekking over wildflower-covered heights. The highest peak and most popular trek is the Liakoura. The truly ambitious can trek via Delphi by starting from Arachova very early in the morning, although this requires a guide. The best starting point for most hikes is the Greek Alpine Club refuge at 1,900 m (6,230 ft), 20 km (12 miles) north of Arachova. ✪ Map R1 • Trekking Hellas: 210 331 0323 • Parnassos Ski Centre: 226 704 2767

Delphi

Galaxidi

Delphi
9 The centre of the world, as Zeus divined by releasing two eagles from opposite ends of the universe and seeing where they crossed. Great mystic powers are associated with this site, whose jutting mountain, gaping chasms and rushing springs indicate a place of dramatic geological upheaval. In ancient times, priestesses communed with the Oracle of Delphi, which gave famously abstruse prophecies. Apollo won dominion over the Oracle, and the site is full of temples to the god and prophets. *(See p114.)*

Galaxidi
10 Pretty Galaxidi is a chic but low-key resort on the Gulf of Corinth that makes a great coastal base for visiting Delphi. Its location between turquoise waters and green mountains makes it tranquil and idyllic, except on summer weekends when Athens' fashionable crowds pack the trendy cafés. Otherwise, take the time to explore its good beaches and 19th-century mansions.
§ Map Q1 • Tourist office: 226 504 1222
• Several buses daily from Terminal B

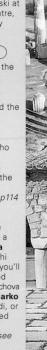

A Driving Trip from Athens to Delphi

Day One

Set out from Athens, breaking up the three-hour drive to Delphi with stops at the scenic monasteries of **Dafni** *(see p111)* and **Osios Loukas**.

Close to Delphi, you might want to stay either at the seaside town of **Galaxidi**, if it's summer, or in the snowy mountain village of **Arachova** in winter. If the former, check into the charming Ganimede hotel and spend the late afternoon at the beach; if the latter, consider staying in a family chateau at the fabulous **Elatos Resort** *(see p146)*. Here, you can take the afternoon to ski at the Parnassos Ski Centre, or to explore the many mountain trails.

Day Two

The next day, head to the ancient site of **Delphi** bright and early. You'll want to spend a lot of time wandering around the **Temple of Apollo**, wondering about the strange rituals of the ancient priestesses who communed with the Oracle. Be sure not to miss the **museum** or the nearby **Sanctuary of Athena Pronaia** *(see p114 for Delphi's sights)*.

If you are in a hurry to return to Athens, grab a quick snack at **Taverna Vakhos** *(p115)* in Delphi before leaving. If not, you'll find more sophisticated fare at Galaxidi and Arachova – try the mussels at **Barko tis Maritsas** in Galaxidi, or the sausages and grilled formaella cheese at Arachova's **Karaouli** *(see p115 for both)*.

Left **Mount Parnassos** Right **Delphi theatre**

Sights in Delphi

1 Sacred Way
This road retraces the route Apollo first followed to Delphi and ends at the temple dedicated to him. The view, of Mount Parnassos looming above and the plunging gorge below, is suitably humbling.

2 Temple of Apollo
This temple contained the *omphalos* (navel-stone), marking the centre of the world, as well as the Oracle. Nearly all ancient authors mention how rulers from throughout the inhabited world sent envoys with lavish offerings to hear the Oracle's prophecies.

3 Sifnian Treasury
This temple-like marble structure, built by envoys from Sifnos, was the richest and most beautiful of several similar treasuries, all constructed as offerings to the Oracle. Its statues are now displayed in the museum.

4 Athenian Treasury
The Athenians decorated their offering with elegant friezes depicting their hometown heroes Theseus and Herakles. The latter's famous Twelve Labours were performed at the Oracle's behest.

5 Theatre
Built in the 4th century BC, this is one of the best preserved theatres of ancient Greece. It also offers a sweeping view of the whole site, especially the dramatically varied landscape that makes Delphi feel so sacred.

6 Roman Agora
This marketplace area was lined with stalls selling sacred objects, where visitors could buy last-minute offerings to the Oracle.

7 Sanctuary of Athena Pronaia
The sanctuary to warrior-goddess Athena was believed to protect the Sanctuary of Apollo from invaders. Though many of the buildings have been destroyed, those that survive are among the finest examples of ancient Greek architecture.

8 Sanctuary of the Earth Goddess
This rock circle surrounding an opening in the earth celebrated the earliest deity associated with the Delphic Oracle: the matriarchal earth goddess. The tradition of the Oracle and priestesses continued, but the ruling deity later become Apollo.

9 Castalian Spring
Though now mostly dry, this spring was where pilgrims cleansed themselves before entering the holy site. You can still see the elaborate fountain-house built around it.

10 Museum
The fantastic museum houses the greatest offerings brought to the Oracle from around the world. ✆ 22650 82312 • Summer: 7:30am–6:45pm daily; Winter: 8:30am–3pm daily • Adm

Delphi's sights are spread over an area of about 2 km (1 mile) and require a day to view In full; admission charge to main site

Price Categories

For a three-course	€	under €30
meal for one with half	€€	€30–€40
a bottle of wine (or	€€€	€40–€50
equivalent meal), taxes	€€€€	€50–€60
and extra charges.	€€€€€	over €60

Left **Taverna Vakhos, Delphi** Right **Kaplanis restaurant, Arahova**

Places to Eat North of Athens

1 Taverna Vakhos
Though Delphi's sites and scenery are fantastic, the same cannot be said for its culinary offerings. This family-run establishment is the exception. It cooks good taverna fare accompanied by views across the Corinthian Gulf. ⊗ *Apollonos 31, Delphi • Map Q1 • 2265 083 186 • €*

2 Topiki Gefsi
Respectable taverna food and a nice view, even if the service does leaves something to be desired. ⊗ *Pavlou 19 & Frederikis, Delphi • Map Q1 • 2265 082 480 • €*

3 Barko tis Maritsas
A most popular taverna, open year round on the beach. Mussels are the local speciality – baked, fried or served in sauce. The homemade vegetable pies are also good. ⊗ *Ianthis, Amfissa, Galaxidi • Map Q1 • 2265 041 059 • €*

4 Taverna Porto
This waterfront taverna makes a good stop after a day of swimming. Feast on large plates of cheap, tasty local seafood. ⊗ *Akti Oianthis 41, Galaxidi • Map Q1 • 2265 041 182 • €*

5 Karaouli
A simple, traditional, delicious taverna. Be sure to try the spicy Arachova sausage and stuffed peppers. ⊗ *Eleftheriou Venizelou, Arachova • Map R1 • 2267 031 001 • Sep–Jun (Sep & Oct: weekends only) • €*

6 Kaplanis
Flavourful taverna classics in a rather fancy room with gilded chandeliers. In spring, be sure to try the fried courgette (zucchini) flowers. Year round, sample the *fromila* (barbecued cheese). ⊗ *Plateia Tropeou, Arachova • Map R1 • 2267 031 891 • €*

7 Babis
A good place to warm up on a cold winter's weekend – the crackling fireplace casts a glow over everything. Go for a bowl of hot, aromatic *stifado* stew (p58). ⊗ *Kalyvia Parnassou, Arachova • Map R1 • 22670 32155 • Open for lunch Oct–Apr daily and for dinner at weekends • €*

8 Emboriko
People come here après ski to warm up with coffee, drinks and snacks. Simple evening meals include pasta, casseroles and steaks. ⊗ *Arachova • Map R1 • 22670 32467 • Open Oct–May all day, but meals served only in the evenings • €*

9 Paradissos
An unpretentious taverna on the road to the northernmost tip of Evia. Enjoy the verdant setting, tender lamb and freshly dug potatoes. ⊗ *Dafni, Evia • Map S1 • 2227 092 172 • €*

10 Kapetanios
Sit by the church and sample a wonderful array of seasonal seafood, raw or fried with cheese. ⊗ *Plateia Ag Tryfonas, Nea Lampsakos, Evia • Map T1 • 22210 28191 • €*

Note: Unless otherwise stated, all restaurants serve vegetarian meals; most tavernas require payment in cash

Left **Mycenae** Centre **Kekhries, Roman harbour** Right **Nafplio street scene**

Into the Peloponnese

OUTSIDE ATHENS, *the Peloponnese is the part of Greece most steeped in myth and history. The Mycenaean kingdoms of Homer's Iliad were once believed to be merely legendary, until 19th-century German archaeologist Heinrich Schleimann unearthed their fabulous palaces on the Argive Peninsula. Now these sites compete with those in Athens as the most important in Greece. But, unlike Athens, the landscapes of those legends – the plains where, according to Homer, great armies assembled, and the fields of Nemea where Herakles wrestled a lion to death – have remained the same for millennia, making this one of the most beautiful regions of Greece, as well as the most fascinating.*

Temple of Zeus, Nemea

Mosaic of Bacchus, Acrocorinth

Sights

1. Corinth Canal
2. Ancient Corinth
3. Acrocorinth
4. Gaia Wines
5. Nemea
6. Mycenae
7. Argos
8. Tiryns
9. Nafplio
10. Epidauros

116

Corinth Canal

The isthmus connecting mainland Greece to the Peloponnese frustrated sailors for thousands of years, forcing them to make long, dangerous journeys around the peninsula. Everyone from Alexander the Great to Roman emperors Nero and Caligula tried digging a canal, but success came only in 1893,

Corinth Canal

when French engineers dynamited their way through the rock. Boats take about an hour to make the 6-km (4-mile) journey. ◎ Map R3

Ancient Corinth

Corinth's location, between the Peloponnese and mainland Greece, made it a rich and powerful trading centre from Mycenaean times onwards. Material wealth was accompanied by a reputation for wild and licentious lifestyles, including polygamy and orgiastic cults, which St Paul addressed with great concern in the biblical Book of *Corinthians*. After the 19th century, Corinth declined into a small, unattractive city. Its attraction resides in the extensive remains of the ancient glories, especially the 6th-century BC Temple of Apollo, and the Roman Agora and Odeon. ◎ Map R3
• *Archaeological sites: summer: 8am–7pm daily; winter: 8am–3pm daily; adm*

Acrocorinth

This towering rock outside Corinth was the strongest natural fortification in ancient Greece. In Archaic times it was crowned by a famous temple to Aphrodite. The structures you see today are mostly medieval Turkish, often having been built over much older buildings. It is a hefty hike to the top, but the effort is rewarded with great views.
◎ *Map R3 • 8:30am–7pm daily • Free*

Gaia Wines

In recent years, the Greek wine industry has been gaining international acclaim, finally bringing serious cultivation techniques to its sun-drenched soils and indigenous grapes. Gaia is one of the best new vineyards, producing deep velvety wines from Nemea's Aghiorghitiko red grapes. ◎ *Koutsi*
• *Map R3 • 27460 22057, 210 8055 642 (call 3 days ahead for a tour and tasting)*

Entrance to Acrocorinth

There are several buses daily to Corinth from Athens' Terminal A, Kifissou 100 (journey time: 90 minutes)

5 Nemea

This was the site of the first labour of Herakles: the slaying of the Nemean lion. The lion's skin was impenetrable, so Herakles strangled the beast, then skinned it and kept its pelt as a coat of armour. This is one of several legends connected with the founding of the Nemean Games, which formed part of the Panhellenic Games. The highlight of Nemea is walking through the great stadium where the contests took place. ⦿ Map R3 • 8:30am–3pm daily • Adm

6 Mycenae

Legend and history combine alluringly at Mycenae. Homer wrote of Agamemnon, Greece's most powerful king during the Trojan War, commanding the citadel of "well-built Mycenae, rich in gold." And history confirms that indeed there was a Trojan War and a powerful civilization based in Mycenae. The evidence came together when Heinrich Schliemann discovered the palace at Mycenae in 1874, much of which accords with Homer's descriptions, including the wealth of gold. ⦿ Map R3 • Summer: 8am–7pm daily; winter: 8am–3pm daily • Adm

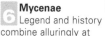

Tiryns' "Cyclopean" walls

7 Argos

Believed to be the longest continually inhabited town in Greece, the modern town sits right on top of the ancient one, leaving much to wonder about but little to see. Fortunately, the 4th-century theatre and excellent museum are well worth visiting, and, if you have a car, drive to the medieval castles of Larissa and Aspis overlooking the plain immortalized by Homer. ⦿ Map R3 • Archaeological site: 8:30am–3pm Tue–Sun; adm

8 Tiryns

This was one of the most important cities of the Mycenaean civilization. Its fortifications of limestone were so massive that later Greeks believed they could have been built only by the giant Cyclops – archaeologists still refer to the walls as "Cyclopean". Although not as grand as Mycenae, Tiryns is better-preserved, especially the ancient palace and great hall. ⦿ Map R3 • Summer: 8am–7pm daily; winter 8am–5pm Mon–Sat; adm

9 Nafplio

Small, seaside Nafplio is one of Greece's most beautiful cities.

Theatre of Epidauros

Nafplio is the best base for exploring the Peloponnese; it is served by several buses daily from Athens' Terminal A, Kifissou 100

Nafplio

For years the Turks and Venetians fought for the city, leaving behind two fantastic hilltop Venetian fortresses and several Turkish mosques. The Greeks seized Nafplio when they won independence in 1821 and made it their first capital, before Athens took that mantle. ◈ Map R3 • Tourist office: Martiou 25, 2752 024 444

Epidauros

The 4th-century BC Theatre of Epidauros is one of the best sites in Greece, marvellously preserved and with astounding acoustics (see pp60–61). Outside the theatre is the sprawling Asklepion, an ancient spa and resort devoted to Asklepios, the god of health. ◈ Map S3 • Summer: 8am–7pm daily; winter: 8am–3pm daily • Adm

---

The Labours of Herakles

Herakles was fathered illegitimately by Zeus. Hera, enraged at her husband's infidelity, drove Herakles mad and caused him to kill his wife. In penance, he was required to perform 12 feats of heroism around the Peloponnese. He was cleansed of his sin and glorified for his feats, which, ironically, are attributed to the jealous goddess: his name means "glory of Hera".

Overnight in Nafplio

Daytime

Visit **Nafplio** on a summer weekend, buying tickets for a performance at ancient **Epidauros** before setting off (see p65).

Take a morning bus from Athens' Terminal A, having also booked a hotel in advance. The nicest place to stay is Nafplia Palace; Pension Acronafplia is more affordable but still good.

Spend the day exploring **Nafplio's Old City**. Buy some drinks and a snack, and take them up to the **Venetian fortress**, which affords glorious views of Nafplio and the Gulf of Argos. If you're feeling fit, climb the 999 steps to the top; otherwise, take a taxi.

Below the fortress, cool off at the small public beach. For more privacy, head down the walkway and go diving from the rocks.

Nighttime

Satiate your hunger at **Kanaris** (p121), returning to the bus station before 7:30pm, when buses depart for **Epidauros**. Even if the performance is in Greek, the powerful acting and magical setting will captivate. Programmes summarize the plot in English. Take the bus back to **Nafplio** and get a good night's sleep.

The following morning, check out, but leave your luggage at the hotel. Take the first bus to **Mycenae** (whose tragic inhabitants may well have been the subject of the previous night's play). Marvel at this legendary prehistoric city for a few hours, then go back to **Nafplio** and hop on a bus back to Athens.

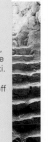

Beyond Athens – Into the Peloponnese

Left **Isthmia** Centre **Waterfall, Loutraki** Right **Kekhries**

🔟 Best of the Rest

Perahora
Though little remains of the Temple of Hera, this is still an idyllic place to come and swim, with a wonderful lighthouse and chapel, and crystal-clear waters. Snorkellers can see ancient ruins underwater. ✎ *Map R2 • Summer: 8am–7pm daily; winter: 8am–3pm • Adm*

Loutraki
Famed for its spring waters, Loutraki is a popular Athenian weekend destination. The top draw is the Hydrotherapy Thermal Spa, though the area is also home to a casino that's said to be one of the biggest in Europe. ✎ *Map R2 • Hydrotherapy Thermal Spa, G Lekka 26, 2744 028 498*

Isthmia
Much of the ancient site has been destroyed, but archaeology fanatics will still want to see the Sanctuary of Poseidon and the stadium that hosted the Panhellenic Games. ✎ *Map R3 • 27410 37244 • 8:30am–3pm daily • Adm*

Kekhries
The site where Theseus defeated the Sinis, the giant who used whole pine trees to sling-shot victims across the water. Today the seaside town makes a nice stop on the beautiful drive to Epidauros. ✎ *Map R3*

Sikia
Along with nearby Xylocastro, this quiet seaside village is a beautiful place to while away an afternoon swimming in clear water, eating freshly caught fish in tavernas scented with flowers, and drinking excellent local wine. ✎ *Map R2*

The Argive Heraion
This sanctuary to goddess Hera, built in the 7th–4th centuries BC, is a wonderfully tranquil spot, with great views over the Argive plain. ✎ *Iraio, S.E. of Nafplio • Map R3 • 8am–5pm Tue–Sun • Adm*

Skoura Wines
Skoura is known for its white wines, especially its deep, fruity chardonnays – a rarity in Greece. Call a few days ahead to arrange a tour and tasting. ✎ *Piryelo, nr Argos • Map R3 • 27510 23688*

Lerna
One of the oldest archaeological sites in Greece, with remains dating back to the fourth millennium BC. ✎ *Map R4 • 8am–3pm Tue–Sun • Adm*

Agia Moni
This 12th-century Byzantine convent and garden makes for a good day out from Nafplio. The nuns sell their own textiles. ✎ *Nr Nafplio • Map R3 • Free*

Asini
This deserted early Helladic settlement is a delightful swimming spot. Nobel Laureate George Seferis thought so, too, in his ode to a place "unknown, forgotten by all, even Homer". ✎ *Map R4*

Taverna Paleo Archontiko, Nafplio

Price Categories

For a three-course meal for one with half a bottle of wine (or equivalent meal), taxes and extra charges.

€	under €30
€€	€30–€40
€€€	€40–€50
€€€€	€50–€60
€€€€€	over €60

Places to Eat

Taverna Paleo Archontiko
Housed in an old mansion, this family-run favourite is usually packed with locals. Nafpliotes go for the excellent rooster cooked in wine, pork stew or rabbit with tomato sauce. ✆ Ypsilandou & Sofroni, Nafplio • Map R3 • 2752 022 449 • €

Kanaris (Karamanlis)
A firm favourite with former president Constantine Karamanlis. Try the stuffed cabbage leaves and yiouvetsi (pasta with roasted meat), washed down with barrel retsina. ✆ Bouboulinas 1, Nafplio • Map R3 • 27520 27668 • €

Spilia
Frequently named as one of the best tavernas in Greece, serving local specialities elevated to their highest culinary potential. Try the braised lamb and baby artichokes, accompanied by wine from local Nemea vineyards. ✆ Tripoleos 165, Kefalari, Argolida (nr Nafplio) • Map R3 • 2751 062 300 • €

O Savas
Savas grows his own avocados, and serves them with everything from roe to mangoes at this green-fruit-focused mezedopleion. ✆ Nea Kios, nr Nafplio • Map R3 • 27510 51425 • €

Mykinaiko
Simple but flavourful classics – stuffed cabbage leaves and aubergine (eggplants) and savoury moussaka – at a small, family-run spot near the ancient site. Once again, don't miss the deep, dark red local Nemean wine. ✆ Mycenae • Map R3 • 2751 076 724 • €

Taverna O Theodorakis
Corinth doesn't have much going for it in the way of restaurants, but Theodorakis does a decent job with seafood, especially sardines and calamari. ✆ Seferi 8, Corinth • Map R3 • 2741 022 578 • €

Restaurant 24 Hours
A stand-by for the wee small hours, with an enormous menu that ranges from taverna fare to schnitzel to pasta. ✆ Agiou Nikolaou 19, Corinth • Map R3 • 2741 083 201 • €

O Kavos
This tiny atmospheric house by the sea serves up far superior fresh grilled fish than any you'll find in Corinth. ✆ Isthmia, 8 km (5 miles) from Corinth • Map R3 • 27410 37906 • €

Maistrali
Popular fish taverna, packed with locals and tourists enjoying huge portions of charcoal-grilled fish and a wide selection of ouzo and tsipouro. ✆ Possidonos 83, Loutraki • Map R2 • 2744 061 699 • €

Leonidas
A popular place for actors as well as audience to stop on the way to or from performances at the ancient theatre. Good pork chops and stuffed vine leaves, and a nice garden at the back. ✆ Main road, Epidauros • Map S3 • 2753 022 115 • €

Left **Glyfada** Right **Ruins at Ramnous**

Around the Attica Coast

FROM AS EARLY AS THE 5TH CENTURY BC, *the ancients built marble temples to their gods and prophets on verdant slopes covered in the dense foliage of dark pines, in a land where the legendary Theseus had once roamed, freeing Attica from a scourge of monsters. Crowning the peninsula, at southernmost Cape Sounio, was the stunning Temple of Poseidon, sparkling like a beacon over the Aegean. Looking at Attica today, it is clear to see that parts of the coast have fallen victim to overdevelopment, but the jewels of Attica remain in the peacefully crumbling temples among the trees, in the best of the region's sandy beaches and in the ultra-luxurious summer clubs, which stretch further south down the coast every year.*

TOP 10 Sights

1. Glyfada
2. Vouliagmeni
3. Lake Vouliagmeni
4. Temple of Poseidon
5. Sanctuary of Artemis, Vavrona
6. Rafina
7. Marathonas
8. Schinias
9. Ramnous
10. Sanctuary of Amphiaraos

Vouliagmeni

Lake Vouliagmeni

Temple of Poseidon

Glyfada

Here, a wealthy, overdeveloped beach-resort and flashy nightlife vibe prevails. There are plenty of designer shops and expensive cafés to sit in while sporting new purchases by day, and trendy summer clubs to dance in by night. ◈ Map T3 • Bus E2 or A2 from Athens

Vouliagmeni

A sprawling seaside resort suburb south of Athens, Vouliagmeni is lined with luxury hotels, yacht clubs and pricey pay-per-visit beaches. But the biggest draw for Athenians are the superglam beachside clubs, the centre of nightlife in summer. All are re-created in luscious over-the-top decor each year. Perennial competitors in the desirability stakes are Island, Tango and Spa. ◈ Map T3 • Bus E22 from Athens

Lake Vouliagmeni

Bathers come year-round to take the warm, therapeutic waters of Lake Vouliagmeni, a large thermal spring that maintains a steady temperature of 22–25˚C (70–77˚F). The source of the clear, half-fresh, half-salt waters is still unknown, but devotees say there's no doubt about their healing properties. It's a great place to swim, especially on cold winter mornings, flanked by a high rock face on one side and trees on the other. ◈ Map T3 • 210 896 2239 • E22 bus from Athens • Summer: 6:30am–8pm; winter: 7:30am–5pm • Adm

Temple of Poseidon

The 5th-century BC temple is one of the few ever built to Poseidon. After watching the sunset from the remaining white marble pillars of this ancient site on the peak of Cape Sounio – silhouetted by the incomparable iridescent blue of the Aegean – you may share the sentiments of the poet Byron. He asked the gods simply to "Place me on Suniom's marbled steep, Where nothing save the waves and I, May hear our mutual murmurs sweep, There, swanlike, let me sing and die." *(See also p45.)* ◈ Map T3 • 2292 039 363 • Bus from the KTEL terminal in Athens (2-hour journey time) • Summer & winter: 9am–sunset daily • Adm

Temple of Poseidon

Sanctuary of Artemis, Vavrona

you're brave enough, climb up on rocks abutting the beach and join the local children in adrenaline-rush cliff-diving. ⬥ Map T2 • KTEL bus from the terminal on Mavromateon

Marathonas
In 490 BC, the Marathon plain was the site of one of history's most important battles. There, an army of 10,000 Greeks and Plataeans defeated 25,000 Persians, preserving the newly founded first democracy. A tomb to the 192 Greek soldiers who fell (in comparison to 6,000 Persians) still stands here. After the victory, Pheidippidis ran the 42 km (26 miles) to Athens to announce the outcome, then collapsed dead on the spot. A museum here displays finds from the area. ⬥ Map T2 • Marathon tomb: 2294 055 462 • Archaeological Museum: 2294 055 155 • 8:30am–3pm Tue–Sun (for both) • buses daily from Mavromateon terminal • Adm (for both)

Sanctuary of Artemis, Vavrona
This temple to Artemis, goddess of the hunt and childbirth, was once the most sacred in Attica. Its highlight was the bear festival, where young girls dressed as cubs performed the "bear dance" in honour of the goddess's favourite animal. When King Agamemnon sacrificed his daughter Iphigenia to Artemis, the goddess saved her and brought her here, where she became a high priestess. Her tomb is the oldest cult shrine on the site. Today the well-preserved site remains green and tranquil. Its museum displays cult finds.
⬥ Markopoulo, Mesogia • Map T3 • 8:30am–3pm Tue–Sun • Adm

Rafina
If you go to the islands of Andros or Evia, you'll spend time in Rafina, Attica's second-largest port after Piraeus. It's smaller and cleaner than its chaotic big brother, but still bustling, filled with fish joints and hawkers. If you have a few hours to kill, take the small bus from the port to the decent beach, which also has a bar. If

Monument at Marathonas

Schinias
Many consider Schinias the most beautiful beach area in Attica, its white-sand coast hugged by dark pine forests. However, the area is undergoing huge changes for the 2004 Olympics, which include building an artificial lake, and possibly archaeological and environmental parks. This means many tavernas are springing up on the once-pristine shore. But with a car it's still possible to find many lovely spots to swim along the coast here, especially mid-week.
⬥ Map T2 • KTEL bus from the Mavromateon terminal

Pines on Schinias beach

9 Ramnous

The ruins of these temples to Nemesis (goddess of divine retribution) and Thetis (Achilles' mother and goddess of law) are among Greece's most unspoiled sites, in a romantically isolated and overgrown grotto with an alluring sea view. Nearby are some beautiful secluded beaches.
◈ *Map T2 • 8:30am–3pm daily • Adm*

10 Sanctuary of Amphiaraos

Built in the 4th century BC, this shrine was both an oracle and health resort. It honoured Amphiaraos, an Argonaut prophet who was tricked into fighting against Thebes, even though he foresaw that he would be killed. In the retreat, he was swallowed by the earth, and reincarnated as a demi-god, returning at this site. In spring, this gladed site is blanketed with flowers. ◈ *Map T2 • 8:30am–3pm Tue–Sun • Adm*

The Local Hero

Theseus is linked with Attica through a mix of mythology and enticing traces of historical evidence that suggest that a King Theseus may have actually existed. This king managed to unite the region's splinter states, while the reputation of Theseus the hero rests on tales of his slaying monsters and bedding everyone from Helen of Troy to Hippolyta, Queen of the Amazons.

A Tour of Attica

Morning

Start early with a drive out of Athens to **Marathonas**. Survey the plain where the Greeks won history's greatest military victory, and pay homage at the warrior's tomb. Then head to the romantic ruins of **Ramnous**, ideally concentrating more on the scenery than the site's original purpose: praying for revenge.

Drive south down the coast, stopping in Loutsa for a grilled fish lunch at **Xypolitos** (see p127).

Afternoon

After lunch, continue south to the well-preserved **Sanctuary of Artemis** at Vavrona, dedicated to the huntress goddess. From there it's a little over an hour's drive to one of Greece's most splendid sights: the **Temple of Poseidon** at Sounio (p123). If there's still plenty of daylight, first head to one of the two nearby beaches. The one on the left of the temple requires an athletic scramble down but offers scenic seclusion; the hotel beach on the right is easily accessible but covered with sun loungers. An hour or two before sunset, wander up to the temple, and watch as twilight deepens the Aegean to purple and the marble columns turn to pink and gold.

Returning to the coastal drive to Athens, consider two dinner options. The nearby taverna **Syrtaki** or, closer to the city, the elegant seaside club **Island**, where you can end your day of beautiful scenery with a vista of beautiful people (see p127 for both).

Left **Aegina harbour** Right **Poros town**

Nearby Islands

1 Salamina
Wooded Salamina has a rich history – playwright Euripides was born here, and in 480 BC, the Greeks famously beat Xerxes here. Its proximity to the industry around Piraeus makes it less popular today. ◎ *Map S3*

2 Aegina
An easy and rewarding day trip, only half an hour from Athens, with pleasant beaches, famously tasty pistachios, the Temple of Aphaia, and Agios Nektarios, one of the largest churches in the Balkans. ◎ *Map S3*

3 Angistri
This tiny islet off Aegina is even more of an escape from it all. Quiet beaches, clear beautiful water, a handful of small hotels and fish tavernas, and not much else. ◎ *Map S3*

4 Hydra
Lovely Hydra town, its cobbled paths winding among old mansions clustered around the clear-watered harbour, is one of Greece's most beautiful spots. Its popularity as a celebrity get-away and movie backdrop hasn't dampened its charm. ◎ *Map S4*

5 Poros
Overlooked by most tourists, Poros is famous for its fragrant lemon groves. Pass over Poros town to walk in the dark woods and bright groves of Kalavria. ◎ *Map S4*

6 Spetses
Popular with British tourists, Spetses offers pine forests, good beaches and a charming harbour town. Cars are banned, but fun water taxis can take you around the coast. ◎ *Map S4*

7 Tzia
Although only half an hour from Lavrion, Tzia remains peaceful and relatively untouristed. Its interior is fertile and flowered. Don't miss the stone Lion of Tzia, carved into a hillside, or the excellent local wine. ◎ *Map U3*

8 Andros
A favourite of Greece's shipping magnates; golden-beached Andros is lovely, exclusive, and expensive. The Goulandris Museum of Modern Art holds world-class exhibits every summer. ◎ *Map V3*

9 Kythnos
Mostly barren and much less picturesque than the other Cyclades, Kythnos does have one thing going for it: healing thermal springs at Loutra that are said to be the best in all the Aegean. ◎ *Map U4*

10 Evia
Huge Evia is the perfect island for hikers, with green mountains and long trails winding through inland villages. At the northern tip, posh resorts cluster around restorative thermal springs. (See p111.)

Boats to Evia and Andros leave from Rafina, boats to Tzia from Lavrio; all other islands listed are served by boats from Piraeus

Price Categories

For a three-course meal for one with half a bottle of wine (or equivalent meal), taxes and extra charges.	€ under €30
	€€ €30–€40
	€€€ €40–€50
	€€€€ €50–€60
	€€€€€ over €60

Syrtaki, Sounio

🔟 Places to Eat

1 Moita, Hydra
Light, creative Mediterranean cuisine in a lovely courtyard. The focus is on seafood, but don't miss the pears poached in wine for dessert. ⊗ *Map S4 • 2298 052 020 • Greek Easter–October • €€€*

2 Vassilis, Mati
Simple taverna serving such delights as a mouth-watering roasted baby pork and *kolokeftedes* (fried courgette balls). ⊗ *27 km of Marathonos Ave, Mati • Map T2 • 2294 033 807 • Greek Easter–Oct daily; Fri and weekends year round • €*

3 Kavouri, Nea Makri
Top-notch taramasalata and fresh grilled seafood (the squid is especially good) at this garden taverna by the sea. ⊗ *Marathonas Beach, Nea Makri • Map T2 • 2294 055 243 • Apr–Oct: daily; Fri & weekends year round • €€*

4 Mezedopoleio To Steki, Aegina
Located near the fish market, you can always be sure there will be good seafood here, accompanied by ouzo. ⊗ *Pan Irioti 45, Aegina • Map S3 • 2297 023 910 • €*

5 Patralis, Spetses
Dull surrounds but probably the widest variety of fresh fish on the island. ⊗ *Kounopitsa, Spetses • Map S4 • 2298 072 134 • €*

6 Syrtaki, nr Sounio
The most popular taverna around Sounio, and with good reason. The shaded three-storey seating area has a nice view of the sea, and spit-cooked beef and octopus are reliably tasty. ⊗ *2 km (1 mile) N of the Temple of Poseidon • Map T3 • 2292 039 125 • €€€*

7 Ennea Kores, Tzia
Bypass other tavernas lining the port and head to the end of the bay and this favourite of the Athenian cognoscenti. Enjoy the view over a *poikilia* (mixed plate) of fresh seafood and veggie treats. ⊗ *Vourkari port, Tzia • Map U3 • €*

8 Xypolitos, nr Vavrona
This coastal fish taverna has great starters, including a nice, light taramasalata – but save room for the grilled fish. ⊗ *25th Martiou and George Papandreou, between Artemida and Loutsa • Map T3 • €€*

9 Ithaki
Elaborate cuisine and glitzy clientele in a wood-and-glass building built into a cliff overlooking the sea. Mainly fish but also a decent choice of meat dishes. ⊗ *Apollonos 28, Vouliagmeni • Map T3 • 210 896 3747 • €€€€*

10 Island, Varkiza
Ritzy Athenians don't mind driving well over an hour out of the city to reach this beautiful seaside club. The Mediterranean fusion food and sushi are only part of it – stay on to enjoy the late-night dancing. ⊗ *27th km on the Athens–Sounio road, Varkiza • Map T3 • 210 965 3563 • May–Oct • €€€€*

➡ *Note: Unless otherwise stated, all restaurants accept credit cards and serve vegetarian meals*

STREETSMART

ATHENS' TOP TEN

Left **Street sign in Greek and Latin scripts** Right **Passengers arriving at Athens Airport**

TOP 10 Planning Your Visit

1 Passport and Visa Information

Citizens from EU countries (plus Norway and Iceland) need only a valid passport to enter Greece, and EU nationals can stay indefinitely. Likewise, US, Canadian, Australian and New Zealand citizens need only a valid passport for entry, and can stay for up to 90 days. Remember that a fine will be imposed if you stay longer without obtaining a visa extension.

2 When to Go

As Athens is a major cultural centre, tourists come and go the year round. In summer, many visitors pass through the city on their way to the islands, though this is certainly not the best time to visit: it's very hot and packed with foreign excursion groups. Try to come in either late spring or early autumn, when you can expect mild weather and a more relaxed atmosphere.

3 Climate

Athens is blessed with a typical Mediterranean climate. Summers are hot, dry and sunny, with temperatures between 22°C (72°F) and 32°C (90°F) throughout July. Winters tend to be mild, with average temperatures ranging from 7°C (44°F) to 13°C (55°F) throughout January, with a fair amount of rain and even occasional snow.

4 What to Take

In summer, light clothing will suffice, but remember to include items with long sleeves and either trousers or a skirt so you can cover up respectably for visiting the churches. Through the rest of the year, you'll need warmer clothing. Be sure to take comfortable walking shoes.

5 Language

Greek is the official language, though many people, especially youngsters and those working in tourism, speak good English. By and large you shouldn't have any problem communicating, but learning a few basic Greek words shows good will on your part.

6 Street and Shop Signs

Street signs are posted in both Greek and Latin (English alphabet) script, and tourist maps are published using the Latin script. However, shops and restaurants, especially those less frequented by tourists, may have signs in Greek only.

7 Health Matters

Citizens from EU countries have the right to free basic medical care with an EHIC (European Health Insurance Card). Travellers from Australia, New Zealand, Canada and the US are not covered by the Greek health system, and will be required to pay for all treatment, except emergency casualty visits.

8 Security

Athens is still one of the safest cities in Europe. Take the usual precautions: lock your car, keep valuables in a safe place and look after your wallet and passport.

9 Local Prices

Greeks complain that living costs have risen substantially since the introduction of the Euro. Expect to pay prices similar to those in other EU countries, except for taxis and public transport, which are cheaper in Athens than in other European capitals.

10 Driving Licences

For car and moped hire, EU citizens need only a national driving licence, but visitors from the US, Canada, Australia and New Zealand are required to show an International Driving Licence before taking to the roads.

Greek National Holidays

1 & 6 January
25 March
First Monday of Lent
Orthodox Easter
1 May
Whit Monday
15 August
28 October
25 & 26 December

Left **Athenian guides** Right **Newspapers**

🔟 Sources of Information

1 GNTO Services
The new Greek National Tourist Board (GNTO) information office, close to Plateia Syntagma, offers basic advice and brochures about the city and the surrounding area.

2 Websites
The GNTO website is a good starting point. For archaeological sites and museums, try browsing www.culture.gr; for forthcoming cultural events www.cultureguide.gr; and for a taste of the Athens Festival summer programme visit www. greekfestival.gr. Greece Now (www.greece.gr) features regular articles about contemporary Greek politics and culture.

3 Newspapers
The English-language papers to look out for are *Athens News* and *Kathimerini*. The former has a section listing forthcoming events; the latter is sold as an insert with the *International Herald Tribune*.

4 Local Magazines
Glossy bi-monthly *Odyssey* features stories about Greece and the Greek diaspora. *Athens Today* is a free fortnightly pocket edition with information for visitors.

5 English-Language Radio and TV
The city radio station Athens 9.84 (9.84FM) broadcasts the news in English at 8:30am and 4:30 pm Mon–Fri, the BBC World Service is on 107.1 FM and most hotels offer satellite TV.

6 Guides and Maps
The GNTO distributes free maps of Central Athens, Piraeus and the coast, and Attica. For the widest range of books about the city in English, try Eleftheroudakis bookshop *(see p91)*.

7 Business Information
The Athens Chamber of Commerce and Industry offers information about business opportunities in the capital, while the British Hellenic Chamber of Commerce provides information about doing business in Greece.

8 Olympic Games
The Olympic movement (www.olympic.org) provides facts and figures from the Athens 2004 Olympics, plus information about past and future games.

9 Disabled Travellers
Organizations such as Holiday Care Service and Tipscope, both based in the UK, provide advice and information for disabled visitors travelling to destinations in Greece. In addition, Can Be Done Tours arranges tailor-made holidays especially for people with disabilities.

10 Background Reading
Beyond the classics listed on page 37, check out *Modern Greece – A Short History* (C M Woodhouse), Petros Haris's *The Longest Night – Chronicles of a Dead City*, which describes life in Athens during World War II, and *Dinner with Persephone* by Patricia Storace – an amusing account of an American poet's one-year sojourn in modern Athens.

Directory

GNTO Offices
- *Greece: Amalias 26, Athens ww.gnto.gr*
- *UK: 4 Conduit St, London (020) 7495 9300 www.gnto.co.uk*
- *US: Olympic Tower, 645 Fifth Avenue, New York (1212) 4215777, www.greektourism.com*
- *Canada: 1500 Don Mills Rd, suite 102, Toronto (1416) 9682220*
- *Australia: 37–49 Pitt St, Sydney (431) 924 11 663*

Business Information
- *British Chamber of Commerce ww.bhcc.gr*
- *Athens Chamber of Commerce and Industry www.acci.gr*

Disabled Travellers
- *Holiday Care Service www.holidaycare.org.uk*
- *Disability Travel www.disabilitytravel.co.uk*
- *Can Be Done Tours (020) 8907 2400 www.canbedone.co.uk*

Streetsmart

Left **Ferry at Piraeus** Right **Athens' taxis**

Arriving in Athens

1 Flights from Europe

Greece's national airline, Olympic Airways, operates direct flights between Athens and most major Europe cities, including London; British Airways and easyJet also operate daily flights from London to Athens (from Heathrow and Gatwick, respectively).

2 Flights from Outside Europe

Greece's national airline, Olympic Airways, operates flights to the Middle East, as well as to Bangkok, Johannesburg, Melbourne, Montreal, Sydney and Toronto. In the US, New York offers the most direct flights to Athens, with Delta flying daily.

3 Finding the Cheapest Flights

For late deals, check out www.lastminute.co.uk and www.bargainflights. com. Some websites, such as www.travelocity. com, will alert you by email when tickets fall below a certain price.

4 Getting from the Airport to the City

Metro Line 3 runs from the airport to Syntagma in the city centre. In addition, three 24-hour express bus services cover the 27-km (18-mile) stretch between the airport and the city: the E94 runs to Ethniki Amyna metro station; the E95 to Plateia Syntagma and the E96 to Piraeus.

Taxis are also readily available, and the journey takes approximately 40 minutes.

5 Ferry from Italy

Though there are no direct ferries from Italy to Piraeus, regular overnight services run from Trieste, Venice, Brindisi, Ancona and Bari to Patra. Most companies then lay on a connecting coach from Patra to Athens. Alternatively, the Hellenic Railways Organization (OSE) operates eight trains daily from Patra to Athens (journey time: 4 hours).

6 Ferry from Cyprus

Ferries run from Limassol in Cyprus (journey time approx 44hrs) to the Athens port of Piraeus.

7 Ferry from Greek Islands to Piraeus

There are regular ferries from the Dodecanese, Cyclades, Saronic Gulf Islands, Crete, Samos and northeastern Aegean Islands to Piraeus. Many islands are also connected to Piraeus by Hellenic Seaways' Catamarans – faster but expensive.

8 Train

There are international trains to Greece from Bulgaria, the Former-Yugoslav Republic of Macedonia (FYROM) and Turkey. These terminate at Thessaloniki, where you will need to change trains for Athens, to arrive at Larissa Station.

9 Overland by Car

Major roads linking Greece to its neighbours run to Thessaloniki: The E90 from Turkey; the E79 from Bulgaria; and the E75 from the FYROM. From Thessaloniki, the E75 runs south to Athens. Arriving from Albania, the border crossing into Greece is at Kakavia. From here, take the regional road to Ioannina, the E92 to Larissa, then the E75 south to Athens.

10 Overland by Bus

The Hellenic Railways Organisation (OSE) also operates daily international bus services to and from Albania and Bulgaria from the Peloponnese train station in Athens. Top Deck is a popular choice with young travellers, they offer a 20-day trip to Greece.

Directory

Airlines
www.olympic-airways.gr
www.britishairways.com
www.easyjet.com
www.delta.com

Airport Information
Athens International Airport 24-hour call centre: 210 353 0000, www.aia.gr

Ferries
www.hellenicseaways.gr
www.greekferries.gr
www.dolphins.gr

Trains & Buses
www.osenet.gr
www.topdecktours.co.uk

Left **Bus** Centre **Metro sign** Right **The funicular**

🔟 Getting Around

On Foot
All the main monuments are concentrated in the city centre, which focuses on busy Plateia Syntagma and can easily be negotiated on foot. From here, you can use the hilltops of the Acropolis and Lykavittos Hill as orientation points.

Tram
There are three tram lines connecting the city centre and the coast: T1 runs from Syntagma to Neo Faliro; T2 from Neo Faliro to Glyfada; and T3 from Glyfada to Syntagma.

Bus
The bus network is extensive. Blue buses run daily 5am–12:30am (there is a limited night service); although cheap, they are often rather crowded. Tickets, which can be bought from most street kiosks (periptera), should be validated in an orange machine upon boarding. You can buy monthly passes covering the entire urban network. A sightseeing bus starts from and terminates in front of the National Archaeological Museum.

Trolleybus
The network has been through a process of expansion and there are 25 routes covered by yellow trolleybuses. Use the same tickets as for blue buses, and validate them upon boarding.

Metro
The metro runs from 5:30am to midnight. Line 1 runs north to south between Kifissia and Piraeus. Line 2 runs from Agios Antonios to Agios Dimitrios, stopping close to the Acropolis en-route, while Line 3 runs from Egaleo to the Eleftherios Venizelos airport, passing through Syntagma en-route.

Car Hire
It's not worth hiring a car while in Athens, though you may want one for exploring the regions beyond the city. Regulations vary from company to company, but you should be over 21 years old and hold a valid driving licence (see also p130).

Parking
Parking in central Athens is a nightmare. The most central (but often very crowded) car park is at Plateia Klafthmonos. Failing that, if your hotel doesn't have parking space, you're probably better off using the out-of-town car park at the new Olympic Stadium in Irini, and taking the metro.

Taxis
Athens' taxis are bright yellow, plentiful and cheap. They can be ordered by phone for a small surcharge, or waved down in the street. En-route, it's quite normal for a driver to pick up extra passengers who are heading in your direction. Fares are higher between midnight and 5am, and you also pay extra for luggage and trips to the airport.

Mopeds
A speedy and fun way to zip around is by moped. If you have a valid driving licence, you can rent one from Rent Moto in Koukaki.

Funicular
One of the best places for watching the sunset over Athens is the summit of Lykavittos Hill (see pp52 & 97). If you don't feel up to the hike, take the funicular from Aristippou. It runs every 20 minutes from 9am to 3am.

Directory

Athens Urban Transport Organisation
www.oasa.gr

Car hire
Avis www.avis.gr

Budget www.budget.gr

Europcar
www.europcar.com

Hertz www.hertz.gr

Moped hire
Moto Rent 210 923 4939, www.motorent.gr

Tram
www.tramsa.gr

Metro
www.ametro.gr

Left **Post boxes** Centre **Public phone booths** Right **Internet café**

Banking and Communication

Currency
Greece adopted the Euro (€) in 2002. The currency is available in denominations of €10, €20, €50 and €100 notes, while coins come in 1, 2, 5, 10, 20, 50 cent (*lepta* in Greek) pieces, as well as larger coins worth €1 and €2.

Banks, ATMs, Cards and Cash
Banks are normally open Mon–Thu 8am–2pm and Fri 8am–1:30pm. ATMs are plentiful in Athens for round-the-clock access to cash. Credit cards are accepted in larger hotels, restaurants and shops, but you will find that less touristy businesses, such as local tavernas, accept cash only.

Post
Airmail letters and postcards take about 4 days to reach other EU countries, and around 10 days to the US, Australia and New Zealand. The most central post office is on Mitropoleos, close to Plateia Syntagma, and works Mon–Fri 7:30am–8pm, Sat 7:30am–2pm, Sun 9am–2pm. Other post offices around town are open Mon–Fri 8am–2pm. Post boxes are yellow and have separate slots for national and international mail.

Telephones
You can make international calls from the Greek Telecommunications

(OTE) offices at Patission 85 (open 24 hrs) and Stadiou 15 (Mon–Fri 7am–midnight, Sat–Sun 8am–midnight). It is also possible to call from telephone booths around town – for these you will need a phone card worth 100 units (€4), which can easily be bought at any street kiosk.

Calling Greece
If you are calling from outside the country, the international code for Greece is 0030, while the area code for Athens is 210.

Greek Telephone Numbers
All Greek numbers now have a total of ten digits, including the area code, which you should use even when dialling from within the respective area.

Mobile Phones
All Greek mobile numbers begin with 69 and have a total of ten digits.

Internet Cafés
Cafés with web access are springing up all over the city. The best in the central area are Museum Internet Café (www.museumcafe.gr) at Patission 46, next door to the National Archaeological Museum, Cafe4u (www.cafe4u.gr) at Ippo-kratous 44 in Exarcheia, which is open 24 hrs and Bits and Bytes at

Akadimias 78, close to Omonia. In Piraeus, try Netmania (www. netmania.gr) at Vasileos Pavlou 135, below Kastella.

Business Facilities
The Athenaeum Inter-Continental and the Hilton (see p141 for both) have well-equipped business centres with telephones, fax machines, internet connection, printers and photocopiers, as well as secretarial and translation services.

Greek Language Courses
The most highly regarded language schools for learning Greek are the Athens Centre and the Hellenic American Union. Both of these schools offer courses of varying duration (3–10 weeks) and intensity.

Directory

Directory Enquiries
• *Greek Directory Enquiries: 131*
• *International Directory Enquiries: 139 (English-speaking); can be used for collect calls*

Athens Centre
• *Archimidous 48*
• *210 701 2268*
• *www.athenscentre.gr*

Hellenic American Union
• *Massalias 22*
• *210 368 0000*
• *www.hau.gr*

Left **Flea market** Right **Gallery shop**

◉10 Shopping Tips

Shopping Areas
The capital's chic designer boutiques line the streets of Kolonaki, with shoe emporia and high street chains on Ermou and Patission. The bargain market areas are Monastiraki, Psiri and Thissio. However, some suburbs have recently made challenging bids to the centre's fashion monopoly, and leafy Kifissia in the north hosts a wealth of upmarket designer boutiques and elegant shopping malls filled with expensive imports. In the south, Glyfada boasts a Miami style coastal boulevard containing branches of most of the centre's clothing, shoe, accessory, home decoration and beauty stores.

Opening Hours
As a general rule, shops open 9am–3pm Mon, Wed and Sat; 9am–2:30pm & 5–8:30pm Tue, Thu and Fri. Department stores, shops in tourist areas, florists, bakeries and many larger shops stay open later and often do not close for lunch. Chemists are closed Sat, and street kiosks often stay open until midnight.

Credit Cards
Most Athens shops accept any major credit card (VISA, American Express, Mastercard, Diners Club), although smaller, family-run shops and tavernas may not. In the countryside and on the islands not only do many establishments refuse credit cards, but also cash points are often few and far between. So, if you are planning a day trip from Athens, make sure you take plenty of cash with you.

Sales Tax
VAT of roughly 18% is included in the price of most items bought in Greece; edible produce is taxed at 8.5%.

Refunds
Goods can be exchanged with a receipt. Although Greek law states that a refund must be given if a customer is dissatisfied with an item purchased, in practice shops will always offer an exchange instead.

Markets
Sunday is the day for Athens' flea market (see p80) and the flea market in Piraeus (see p105). Additionally, each area of Athens holds its own weekly street market, the laiko, at which local residents purchase fresh fruit, vegetables, fish and even underwear.

Sales
Jan/Feb and August are the proper sales months, but you will find shops with prosfores (discounts) throughout the year. Stock shops such as The Factory Outlet on Pireos (running between Plateia Omonia and Piraeus) has a wide range of designer brands at bargain prices.

Souvenirs
Plaka and Monastiraki are the best areas for traditional gifts such as handicrafts, vases, leather goods and worry beads aplenty, as well as more contemporary pieces by young Greek artists. The area around Athinas is the best place to buy olives and olive oil, Greek cheeses, honey, spices, herbs, tin trays and jugs.

Museum Reproductions
Both the Benaki Museum (pp22–3) and the Museum of Cycladic Art (pp18–19) sell excellent reproductions. The former stocks copies of icons, sculptures and ancient vases, toys and jewellery; the latter trades in wonderful replicas of Cycladic figurines.

Jewellery
Greece is justly renowned for its jewellery. Old masters Lalaounis (pp72 & 73) and Zolotas (p91), both famous for intricate works in gold, have showrooms on Voukourestiou, alongside international brands like Bulgari and Gavello. Newer talents, such as Elena Votsi (p55) and Lito Karacostanoglou are based in chic Kolonaki. Global high street jeweller and watchmaker Folli Follie (p99) has boutiques in most upmarket retail areas of Athens.

⟶ *For the best places to shop in Athens* **see pp54–5**

Streetsmart

Left **A Plaka taverna** Right **Ouzeri**

Dining in Athens

1 Estiatorion
Most of the dishes on offer in an *estiatorion* are oven-baked meat and fish specialities, such as moussaka (layers of aubergine and minced meat) *stifado* (stew) and *gemista* (stuffed vegetables), which are often prepared in advance and served luke-warm. Deserts are normally limited to sweet pastries and fresh fruit.

2 Taverna
Classic taverna fare is mezes (hors-d'oeuvres), which can be served hot or cold, plus freshly fried or grilled meat and fish dishes. In some establishments there is no menu, but waiters bring round trays laden with dishes on offer, so you can choose what you like the look of. There are no set courses, and plates tend to arrive in a steady, if somewhat random, stream.

3 Psistaria
A carnivore's paradise, a *psistaria* specializes in spit-roasts and char-grilling *(sta karvouna)* meats such as *souvlaki* (shish kebabs), *kokoretsi* (offal) and spit-roast lamb and chicken. Vegetarians are not entirely un-catered for, and can opt for an assemblage of basic side dishes: *horiatiki salata* (Greek salad), *tzatziki* (yoghurt and cucumber dip), *saganaki* (fried cheese) and *tiganites patates* (chips).

4 Psarotaverna
A psarotaverna specializes in freshly caught local fish such as *barbouni* (red mullet) and *xifias* (swordfish). They are normally barbecued and served with lemon and olive oil. Starters might include *kalamarakia* (baby squid), *okhtapodhi* (octopus) and *garidhes* (shrimps).

5 Ouzeries and Mezedopoleia
Taking its name from the strangely uplifting and highly intoxicating anise-flavoured spirit, ouzo, an ouzeri is the place to visit for relaxed drinking and chatting with friends over a range of mezes. Beer and wine are normally also available. Mezedopoleia offer more substantial mezes that, in their variety and quantity, can form quite a feast. Some of Athens' best are around Omonia *(see p92)*.

6 Snacks
While American-style fast-food chains have made little impression on local eating habits, Greeks are tremendous snackers and happy to satiate their peckishness with *tiropites* (cheese pies), *spanakopites* (spinach pies) and takeaway *souvlaki* (pitta bread filled with barbecued meat, tzatziki and freshly chopped onion and tomatoes). The Greek chain Everest does tasty, freshly filled toasted sandwiches.

7 Meal times
The majority of Greeks adhere to the age-old tradition of a strong wake-me-up coffee for breakfast, then eat lunch around 3pm and dinner after 10pm. Most restaurants serve lunch between noon and 4pm and dinner from 8pm until midnight, though in touristy areas such as Plaka you'll find that many establishments stay open all day.

8 Dress
Greeks regularly eat out with family and friends and tend to dress informally for such occasions. Although it's best not to turn up in shorts, men are never required to wear ties, even in the smartest restaurants, though Greek women usually dress to impress on a night out.

9 Live music
Many tavernas, particularly in Plaka, lay on nighttime performances of traditional Greek music. They are mainly intended for tourists, but can be lively and entertaining nevertheless.

10 Tipping
It is customary to leave a 10% tip if you have enjoyed your meal and were satisfied with the service. In the week preceding Easter and at Christmas restaurants add on an obligatory 18% to the bill for the waiters.

Left **Street hawkers** Right **Busy street scene**

10 Things to Avoid

1 Getting Ripped Off by Taxi Drivers

Athens' taxis might be cheap but one occasionally hears stories of tourists being overcharged. To avoid this, simply check that the taxi's meter is displayed and that it is switched on at the start of your journey.

2 Pushy Touts

The streets of Plaka are thronged with touts, eager to pull passers-by into restaurants and souvenir shops. To a lesser degree this is true of other city-centre neighbourhoods. Most of these establishments offer perfectly good services, but don't let yourself be bullied into eating or shopping somewhere against your will.

3 Entering Churches in Skimpy Clothes

Respect local customs: even in summer, ensure your shoulders, chest and legs are covered up when visiting churches.

4 Travelling Without a Valid Ticket

Random stop-checks take place on the buses, trams and metro, and failure to display a valid ticket incurs an on-the-spot fine, ranging from €30 to €72.

5 Flushing Paper Down Toilets

The Greek plumbing system has narrow drains that are not adept at dealing with toilet paper: when you use the bathroom, put paper in the white plastic bin provided, not down the toilet. Failure to comply with this rule means running the risk of blocked drains and flooded bathrooms.

6 The Dogs

An estimated 150,000 stray dogs live on Athens' streets. In an effort to limit their multiplication, the city council has set up a sterilization scheme, rather than having them put down. These dogs are generally completely harmless, but can appear alarming when running in packs, especially during the mating season.

7 "No Smoking"

Greeks smoke almost twice as many cigarettes per capita than the European average. In late 2002, smoking was officially banned in all enclosed public spaces, and restaurants were supposed to adopt designated "Smoking" and "No smoking" areas. However, it remains to be seen how seriously Greeks will take this law, so don't count on a smoke-free holiday.

8 Driving In Athens

This is a congested city. There are many one-way streets and pedestrianized streets in the centre, parking is scarce and the Greeks drive with wild abandon. For all these reasons, it is best for visitors to use public transport, taxis and feet (see p133).

9 Feeding Cats When Dining Out

While its very tempting to offer titbits to sad-eyed cats imploring you with soft meows, you are likely to incur the wrath of the restaurateur. Stray cats are all too plentiful, and a major nuisance to Athens' restaurants.

10 Photographing Military Bases

Remember the much-publicized story of the 12 British and two Dutch plane-spotters who were arrested for taking notes at a Greek army airbase in November 2001? They were subsequently imprisoned on spying charges and claim to have spent £25,000 each in legal costs to prove their innocence. All military installations are clearly marked with a sign showing "no cameras": photography and note-taking are strictly forbidden!

Emergencies

General emergencies
- Police 100
- Ambulance 166
- Fire brigade 199

Hospitals
- Hospital/clinics on duty 1434
- Pharmacies on duty 1434

Left **Tour group** Right **Epidauros theatre**

🔟 Specialist Tours

Half-Day Athens Sightseeing

If you're short of time, let a professional guide whisk you through the city's ancient core. Key Tours organize amusing and informative tours, starting from the Kalimarmaro Stadium *(see p95)*, then wending through the city to the Acropolis.

Athens by Night

Fantasy Travel arrange evening bus trips to the sea at Piraeus, stopping at Mikrolimani for an ouzo aperitif overlooking the fishing harbour. Then it's back to the centre for dinner in a Plaka taverna.

Cape Sounio

An afternoon bus tour along the coast southwest of Athens, past the seaside suburbs of Glyfada, Voula and Vouliagmeni, to the stunning clifftop Temple of Poseidon *(see p123)*. There's just time for an early evening drink before a return to Athens.

Evening Cruise to Epidauros Theatre

Epirotiki Tours arrange evening boat trips to Epidauros for an open-air theatrical performance in the ancient theatre Jun–Aug. A candlelit dinner is served aboard on the return journey.

One-Day Cruise of Saronic Islands

Epirotiki Tours' boats depart early morning from Paleo Faliro, then cruise around the islands of Aegina, Poros and Hydra, with a short stop at each. Lunch on board is part of the deal, and you're back in town for the early evening.

Delphi

Key Tours and Fantasy Travel both offer a full-day trip from Athens to the archaeological site of Delphi. After lunch, the tour takes in the picturesque hillside town of Arachova, renowned for its hand-woven rugs and excellent local cheese.

Hiking on Mount Parnitha

For a breath of mountain air, book up with Trekking Hellas for a 4-hour hiking expedition up Mount Parnitha. A professional guide will lead you along a marked route up the craggy Houni ravine from Agia Triada to the Bafi refuge.

One-Day Sailing Trip

Ghiolman Yachts have a fleet of smart boats of various sizes available for tailor-made one-day sailing trips in the company of an English-speaking skipper. This is undoubtedly the best way to explore the islands.

One-Day Diving Trip

The Aegean Dive Center organizes diving trips to a wreck, a cave and a reef along the coast between Glyfada and Cape Sounio.

With water temperatures around 26°C (79°F) in summer and 14°C (57°F) in winter, diving is possible all the year round. The staff speak excellent English, and tuition is available to those with no previous experience.

Helicopter Tours

For a dramatic bird's-eye view of the city, take a helicopter ride with Hop In Zinon. Flights can be arranged throughout the year, and you can choose the route you wish to take. Expect to pay €1750 for up to five people for 30 minutes' flying time.

Directory

- Aegean Dive Center, Zamanou 53, Pandhoras, Glyfada; 210 894 5409; www.adc.gr
- Epirotiki Tours, 210 429 1501; www.epirotikigroup.gr
- Fantasy Travel, Xenofondos 8; 210 322 8410 & 331 0530–3; www.fantasy.gr
- Ghiolman Yachts, Filellinon 14; 210 323 0330; www.ghiolman.com
- Hop In Zinon, Zanni 29, Piraeus; 210 428 5500; www.hopin.com
- Key Tours, Kallirois 4; 210 923 3166 & 923 3266; www.keytours.gr
- Trekking Hellas, Filellinon 7; 210 331 0323; www.trekking.gr

Acropolis at night

Accommodation Tips

1 Choosing a Hotel
The Hellenic Chamber of Hotels have a complete list of hotels in Athens and can make reservations for you. The GNTO *(see p131)* website also has an extensive list of hotels.

2 Websites
The websites listed in the directory are easy to use and book through, and many offer substantial discounts. Many sites selling flights *(see p132)* also offer hotel booking services.

3 Central Accommodation
Athens' suburbs are vast, and if you choose accommodation on the periphery you will waste a lot of time travelling to the main sights. The most centrally located hotels are in the areas of Plaka, Makrigianni, Koukaki, Monastiraki, Thissio and Syntagma.

4 High Season
High season runs from early July to late September. The period from April to June, plus the month of October are mid-season, and low season runs from the beginning of November to the end of March. Seasonal price differences vary from hotel to hotel.

5 Bargaining
For all but the luxury hotels, do not be ashamed to try and agree discounts with the hotel management – it is often possible to bargain for prices lower than those quoted, especially if staying for longer periods during low season.

6 What's Included in the Price?
Quoted prices usually include continental breakfast, a standard 12% service charge, and 10% tax. The use of hotel facilities such as gyms and pools is normally free to guests. Rooms in the better hotels have air conditioning, though in the cheaper places you might have to pay extra for this facility, if it is available at all.

7 Late Arrivals
If you've just got off a plane and need a place to stay, the new Sofitel Athens Airport Hotel is an excellent if rather pricey option *(see p141)*. Alternatively, Plotin Travel (210 353 0440), opposite the Arrivals area, is open 7am–11pm and can help you find reasonably priced accommodation.

8 Single Travellers
If you are travelling alone and looking for cheap accommodation the YHA *(see p145)* is a good bet. A grade or two up, the Marble House Pension *(see p143)* and the Hotel Plaka *(see p142)* both have several single rooms. Otherwise, as a general rule, one person in a double pays the full rate, minus the second breakfast.

9 Disabled Travellers
When booking your hotel, bear in mind that modern hotels tend to be far better equipped. The Hilton and the Athenaeum Inter-Continental both have several rooms specifically designed for disabled travellers.

10 Children
Most hotels allow one or two children (the cut off age varies from 12 to 18) to stay in their parents' double room – the extra beds are free, you just pay for breakfast. Many of the better hotels also offer babysitting.

Directory

Hellenic Chamber of Hotels
• *Stadiou 24; 210 331 0022*
• *Help Desk, Stadiou 24, on the 7th floor; 8am–2pm Mon–Fri*
• *www.grhotels.gr*

Websites
• *www.athens. hotels-nb.com*
• *www.discounthotel reservation.org*
• *www.hollidaycity europe.com*
• *www.totalstay.com*
• *www.placeto stay.com*

Sofitel Athens Airport Hotel
• *210 354 4000*
• *www.sofitel.com*

Left **St George Lycabettus** Right **Athenaeum Intercontinental**

⑩ Luxury and Boutique Hotels

1 King George Palace

This grandiose hotel and former retreat of the rich and famous reopened in 2004 after a 14-year closure. The 104 rooms and suites, all with marble bathrooms, are individually furnished with select antiques. ⊗ *Vas Georgiou A, Syntagma • Map M3 • 210 322 2210 • www.king georgepalace.gr • €€€€*

2 Hotel Grande Bretagne

With its marble lobby, oriental carpets and glittering chandeliers, this grandiose establishment exudes timeless luxury. The opulence continues through 327 rooms and suites, a rooftop restaurant and pool, and the fitness centre. ⊗ *Georgiou 1 • Map M3 • 210 333 0000 • www.grandebretagne.gr • €€€€€*

3 Divani Acropolis

A mere stone's throw from the Acropolis, this hotel is popular with well-heeled Greeks, keen on the profusion of gilt, mirrors and potted palms. Drinks and buffets are served on the roof garden in summer, and there's a preserved section of the ancient Themistoklean Wall in the basement. ⊗ *Parthenonos 19–25, Makrigianni • Map C6 • 210 9280 100 • €€€*

4 Semiramis

Orange, pink and lime-green predominate in this funky 57-room hotel designed by Karim Rashid. There's a heated outdoor pool and a fitness and beauty centre. An ever-changing selection of contemporary art is displayed in the lobby. ⊗ *Harilaou Trikoupi 48, Kefalari, Kifissia • Map T2 • 210 628 4400 • www. semiramisathens.com • €€€€*

5 St George Lycabettus

A chic 157-room hotel, built into the pine-scented slopes of Lykavittos Hill. Full use is made of the rooftop, with an excellent restaurant, a swimming pool and a bar sharing the views. A minibus service will whisk you to Plateia Syntagma. ⊗ *2 Kleomenous, Kolonaki • Map F3 • 210 729 0711 • www.sglycabettus.gr • €€€€*

6 Hotel Pentelikon

In the smart northern suburb of Kifissia, this charming 1920s' building is set in peaceful gardens with a swimming pool. Expanded in 2006, it now has 101 rooms and suites. And then there's the superb Vardis restaurant (see p56). ⊗ *Deligianni 55, Kefalari, Kifissia • Map T2 • 210 623 0650 • www. hotelpentelikon.gr • €€€€€*

7 Life Gallery

An all-glass boutique designer hotel with 30 rooms, studios and suites set in a garden with trees and a pool. The modern, minimalist furnishing is complemented by earthy colours (cream, coffee, grey and beige) and atmospheric lighting. Facilities include the Ananea Health and Spa. ⊗ *Thiseos 103, Ekali • Map T2 • 210 626 0400 • www.bluegr.com • €€€€*

8 Divani Apollon Palace & Spa

A vast seaside hotel, the spacious rooms adorned with oak furniture and marble bathrooms. The complex gives onto a private beach, and there are also out- and indoor pools. A shuttle bus serves Plateia Syntagma. ⊗ *Vouliagmeni • Map T3 • 210 891 1100 • www. divanis.com • €€€€*

9 Astir Palace Resort

Very exclusive seaside resort that's popular with the Greek jet set. The complex encompasses three hotels, private beaches, leisure facilities and sea-water pools. Shuttle buses and limousines provide access to central Athens. ⊗ *Vouliagmeni • Map T3 • 210 890 2000 • www. astir-palace.com • €€€€€*

10 The Margi Hotel

A 5-minute walk from Vouliagmeni beach, this gem of a hotel comprises 81 rooms and 7 suites, decorated in warm hues, with 19th-century antiques and marble bathrooms. The lounge bar is where guests relax in the evenings on poolside sofas. ⊗ *Litous 11, Vouliagmeni • Map T3 • 210 896 2061 • www.themargi.gr • €€€€*

Note: *Unless otherwise stated, all hotels accept credit cards, have en-suite bathrooms and air conditioning (A/C)*

Price Categories

For a standard, double room per night (with breakfast if included), taxes and extra charges.

€	under €100
€€	€100–€150
€€€	€150–€250
€€€€	€250–€350
€€€€€	over €350

Left **Callirhoe** Right **Metropolitan**

Business and High-End Hotels

NJV Athens Plaza
Smack in the centre of town, this hotel has beautiful designer rooms with marble bathrooms, massage showers, Bulgari toiletries, a famously elegant lobby and a 24-hour business centre. Rooms on the eighth and ninth floors have great views of the Acropolis. ⊗ *Vasileos Georgiou & Stadiou • Map M3 • 210 335 2400 • www.classical hotels.com • €€€€*

The Hilton
Having undergone massive refurbishment in 2003, Athens Hilton is typically smart, functional and modern. Ample facilities include six restaurants, two bars (one on the rooftop), a swimming pool and health centre, plus extensive conference amenities. ⊗ *Vasilissis Sofias 46, Ilissia • Map G4 • 210 728 1000 • www1. hilton.com • €€€€€*

Athenian Callirhoe
A new addition, and one with a clear focus on style. The metal-toned, minimalist lobby leads up to rooms that are designer-sleek, sharp and fully fitted out with luxury amenities. Staff seem genuinely eager to make your stay a pleasure. ⊗ *Kallirois 32 & Petmeza • Map C6 • 210 921 5353 • www.tac.gr • €€€*

Metropolitan
Ever popular with executive travellers for its full range of business facilities, 24-hour restaurant and well-appointed rooms – plus extras like free sessions with a personal trainer in the gym. There's a free hourly shuttle to the city centre. ⊗ *Syngrou 385, Delta Falirou • 210 947 1000 • www.chandris.gr • €€€*

Ledra Marriott
Friendly, helpful staff and equally appealing rooms, decorated in warm hues, with nice touches like goosedown duvets and marble bathrooms. The Polynesian Kona Kai restaurant is highly rated and a favourite of business diners. ⊗ *Syngrou 115 • Map T2 • 210 930 0000 • www.marriott.com • €€€*

Athenaeum Inter-Continental
Well-equipped, modern and stylish, if a little lacking in character. The excellent business facilities make it popular with executives, who probably also appreciate the gym, sauna, pool and shuttle to the city centre. ⊗ *Syngrou 89–93, Neos Kosmos • Map T2 • 210 920 6000 • www.inter continental.com • €€€€*

Athens Park Hotel
Overlooking the lush greenery of Pedion Areos Park, this smart hotel has 152 rooms and suites decorated in subtle muted hues, each with a grey marble bathroom. Rooftop pool and fitness centre ⊗ *Leoforos Alexandras 10, Exarhia • Map D1 • 210 889 4500 • www. athensparkhotel.gr • €€€*

Divani Caravel
The lobby is decorated with antiques and marble, the rooms fitted out with every business amenity. There are restaurants and bars, and a rooftop garden with an indoor/outdoor pool. A free shuttle takes you to Syntagma, and 35 of the rooms have Acropolis views. ⊗ *Vasileos Alexandrou 2, Pangrati • Map G5 • 210 720 7000 • www.divanis.com • €€€€*

Fresh Hotel
Close to the gritty Central Market, Fresh brings designer chic to downtown Athens. The 133 rooms have minimalist furniture in vivid oranges, pinks and greens. There is a rooftop café with a small pool. ⊗ *Sophokleous 26 & Klisthenous, Psiri • Map J1 • 210 524 8511 • www.freshhotel.gr • €€€*

Sofitel
Sofitel shatters the perception that airport hotels must be bland. Soundproof rooms are elegant, sophisticated, and packed with amenities. Business and conference facilities are among the best in Greece, and the glassed-in rooftop pool has fascinating runway views. ⊗ *Athens Airport, Spata, Attica • Map T3 • 210 354 4000 • www. sofitel.com • €€€€€*

Left **Esperia Palace** Right **Titania**

Mid-Range Hotels

1 Hotel Plaka
This hotel is great value for its unbeatable location between Plaka and the shopping street of Ermou, and for its warm and simple but stylish rooms. The roof garden looks out to the Acropolis. ✆ *Kapnikareas 7 & Mitropoleos, Monastiraki • Map K3 • 210 322 2706 • www.plakahotel.gr • €€*

2 Electra Palace
Probably the nicest place to stay in Plaka, this stylish, modern hotel has a cleverly constructed mock Neo-Classical façade. The pool on the roof, with an Acropolis view, is a great place to cool off after a day of sight-seeing. ✆ *Navarchou Nikodimou 18, Plaka • Map L4 • 210 337 0000 • www.electrahotels.gr • €€€*

3 Adrian
The Adrian offers rooms that are small, clean and serviceable, if somewhat sterile, in the heart of Plaka next to Hadrian's Library. The rooms have small balconies and the roof garden has lovely views. The café-filled square below is a nice place to sit, but can get noisy at night. ✆ *Adrianou 74, Plaka • Map J3 • 210 322 1553 • www.douros-hotels.com • €€*

4 Acropolis Select
This is one of the best deals in town. For only a little more than most budget hotels, you get a stylish restaurant and lobby, and bright, comfortable rooms with room service, satellite TV, business amenities, and, if you ask, Acropolis views. Though not located in a tourist neighbourhood, it's within an easy walk of most sights. ✆ *Falirou 37–39, Koukaki • Map C6 • 210 921 1610 • www.acropoliselect.gr • €€*

5 Herodion
Located in a quiet neighbourhood just below the Acropolis, this attractive, modern hotel has comfortable, newly decorated rooms, the pale green and light wood accents of which feel cool and relaxing after a day touring the sights. Other features include internet connections in every room and a flower-filled breakfast atrium. ✆ *Robertou Galli 4, Makrigianni • Map C6 • 210 923 6832 • www.herodion.gr • €€€*

6 Amalia
Price and location (on Plateia Syntagma, directly across from the National Gardens) combine admirably. The rooms are comfortable, functional and, despite facing a noisy major road, surprisingly quiet. ✆ *Amalias 10, Syntagma • Map M4 • 210 323 7301 • www.amalia.gr • €€*

7 Athens Cypria
Located just steps away from the bustle of Syntagma and the top-notch shopping of Ermou, the Cypria's recently renovated rooms are clean and comfortable, if a little bland and uniform. A hefty breakfast buffet is served until 10am. ✆ *Diomeias 5, Syntagma • Map L3 • 210 323 8034 • www.athenscypria.com • €€*

8 Best Western Esperia Palace
A good central option for a short stay, located on one of the city's busiest streets. Rooms are quiet and tastefully furnished, and offer a wide range of facilities. Rooms above the seventh floor have Acropolis views. ✆ *Stadiou 22, Panepistimiou • Map L2 • 210 323 8001 • www.esperia.gr • €€€*

9 Titania
Capacious rooms and bathrooms for this price bracket, and the hotel's in a central location too. However, though close to the sights, bear in mind that this is the gritty, rather than glamorous, end of central Athens. ✆ *Panepistimiou 52, Omonia • Map L1 • 210 332 6000 • www.titania.gr • €€*

10 Grand O' Hotel
This contemporary, stylish hotel, with an Art Deco reception area, has 115 rooms and suites decorated in shades of green and lilac. The Omonia Times restaurant has fine views of the city. ✆ *Pireos 2, Omonia • Map C2 • 210 528 2100 • www.classicalhotels.com • €€*

Note: Unless otherwise stated, all hotels accept credit cards, have en-suite bathrooms and air conditioning (A/C)

Price Categories	
For a standard, double room per night (with breakfast if included), taxes and extra charges.	€ under €100
	€€ €100–€150
	€€€ €150–€250
	€€€€ €250–€350
	€€€€€ over €350

Left **Marble House Pension** Right **Art Gallery Hotel**

TOP 10 Budget Hotels

1 Marble House Pension

A favourite of students and artists, Marble House has clean, simple rooms and a friendly attitude. It offers discounted tours and monthly rates in the off season. Guests pay extra for air conditioning and private bath. ❧ *Zini 35A, Koukaki • Map B6 • 210 923 4058 • www.marblehouse.gr • €*

2 Art Gallery Hotel

The priciest of the budget options, but the hotel offers nice wooden floors, art in every room and a short walk to the Acropolis and several good restaurants. There are low monthly rates in the off season. No breakfast served. ❧ *Erethiou 5, Koukaki • Map C6 • 210 923 8376 • €€*

3 Acropolis House

This 120-year-old house right in the middle of Plaka is a favourite with artists and professors who enjoy the quiet, historic location and the original frescoes in the entryway. Rooms are basic and clean, though most have ugly linoleum floors and only half have air conditioning – for which guests pay extra. ❧ *Kodrou 6–8, Plaka • Map L4 • 210 322 2344 • €*

4 Hotel Attalos

It's central, cheap and clean, and if that's all you require then the Attalos is fine. But the rooms are far from suave, their style taking the form of lino, fluorescent lights and dorm-quality furniture. It's located halfway between the colourful Central Market and the anarchic Monastiraki Flea Market. ❧ *Athinas 29, Monastiraki • Map J2 • 210 321 2801 • €€*

5 Cecil Hotel

Just down the street from the Attalos, in the same colourful-cum-seedy district. Quite a different interior, though, in this renovated Neo-Classical mansion, with polished wood floors, high moulded ceilings and bright, cosy furnishings. Still fairly basic, but a cheerful atmosphere prevails. ❧ *Athinas 39, Monastiraki • Map J2 • 210 321 7079 • www.cecil.gr • €*

6 Jason Inn

Excellent value. The Rooms and services are much nicer and more modern than you might expect from the budget bracket, and guests earn high praise for the helpful, friendly service. Though not in a tourist neighbourhood, it's still an easy walk to several sights and good restaurants. ❧ *Asomaton 12, Monastiraki • Map B3 • 210 325 1106 • www.douros-hotels.com • €*

7 King Jason

Similarly turned out sibling of the Jason Inn, so rooms are stylish as well as clean and comfortable. The bar and restaurant are cheerful and pleasant, thankfully, as the run-down neighbourhood doesn't offer much in the way of sustenance. ❧ *Kolonou 26, Metaxourgeio • Map B2 • 210 523 4721 • www.douros-hotels.com • €*

8 Hotel Carolina

Almost exclusively inhabited by students and backpackers, the Carolina has a perpetual international-party vibe. It's a fun place to meet people, but can get noisy at night. Facilities include an Internet corner ❧ *Kolokotroni 55, Syntagma • Map K2 • 210 324 3551 • www.hotelcarolina.gr • €*

9 The Exarcheion

A fixture on the international backpacking circuit for years. Rooms are spare but well kept, prices are cheap, the staff is young and friendly and the small outdoor bar is in the centre of lively, student-filled Plateia Exarcheia. ❧ *Themistokleous 55, Exarcheia • Map D2 • 210 380 0731 • €€*

10 Hotel Dryades

Similar to The Exarcheion in terms of value and the level of facilities, but Hotel Dryades is less central and therefore quieter. It's also located near several modelling agencies, who frequently use the hotel to put up models. ❧ *Dryadon 4, Exarcheia • Map D1 • 210 382 7362 • €*

Left and Right **Brasil Hotel Apartments**

Long-Stay Hotels & Apartments

1 Tony's Hotel
These studios are smaller than many hotel rooms and have cold tile floors. However, they are new and clean, with well-fitted bathrooms and kitchenettes, large balconies and they are a short walk to the Acropolis. ◈ *Zacharista 26, Koukaki • Map B1 • 210 923 0561 • www.hoteltony.gr • €*

2 Holiday Suites
These comfortable suites and studio apartments are run by Holiday Inn, and offer all the services and amenities of that chain. All have large bathrooms, kitchenettes, and a small office area. The location is a short distance from the centre and can be quickly reached by bus or cab. ◈ *Arnis 4, Ilissia • 210 727 8690 • www.holiday-suites.com • €€€€€*

3 Delice Hotel Apartments
These studios, suites and apartments are basic but generously proportioned, with separate bedrooms, kitchens and living areas. The location offers little in the way of sights, restaurants and bars, so you'll need to take a bus to the centre. ◈ *Vasileos Alexandrou 3 & Vrasida, Ilissia • 210 723 8311 • €€€*

4 President Hotel
This is a full-service hotel that rents almost exclusively by the month. Comfortable rooms have most amenities, but no long-stay extras like kitchenettes or living areas. ◈ *Kifissias 43, Ambelokipi • 210 698 9000 • www.president.gr • €€*

5 Blazer Suites
The entire hotel is suites and apartments, a convenience for the long-stay guest. The accommodation is pleasant and simple, and the bathrooms employ a distinct economy of scale. The location is Athens' southernmost suburb – great for clean air, nearby beaches and summer clubs, but a bit of a slog to reach the city centre. ◈ *Karamanli 1–3, Voula • 210 965 8801–7 • www.blazersuites.gr • €€€€*

6 Oasis Hotel Apartments
Another of the many apartment-only hotels in the wealthy southern suburbs. Most of the two-room apartments with kitchenettes have sea views; those that don't overlook the hotel's best advantage, a garden courtyard with a pool and Jacuzzi. All are served by full hotel amenities, including extras like childcare. ◈ *Poseidonos 27, Glyfada • 210 894 1555 • www.oasishotel.gr • €€€*

7 Brasil Hotel Apartments
Located in a quiet residential neighbourhood in the wealthy southern suburb of Glyfada, this hotel offers one and two bedroom apartments with full kitchens and access to all hotel services, including business facilities. The hotel is close to the beach and surrounded by gardens. ◈ *Eleftherias 4, Glyfada • 210 894 2124–6 • www.brasilhotel.gr • €€€€*

8 Oneiro Luxury Apartments
Most of these one- and two-bed apartments are quite luxurious, fitted out with antiques, chandeliers and views of the Saronic Gulf. In addition to a pool, Jacuzzi and business facilities, there are also well appointed public spaces and a garden. ◈ *Psiloriti 98–100, Ano Glyfada • 210 963 3011, 964 6787 • €€€€–€€€€€*

9 AVA Hotels Suites & Apartments
Renovated in the summer of 2004, this boutique hotel offers large suites and apartments with kitchen-ettes. It lies at the foot of the Acropolis, in Plaka. ◈ *Lysikratous 9–11, Plaka • Map L5 • 210 325 9000 • www.avahotel.gr*

10 Apartments Kolonaki
This hotel offers 14 open-plan apartments, all with a balcony, a fully-equipped kitchen and a stylish living room. ◈ *Anapiron Polomou 1 • Map F3 • 210 721 8456 • www.apartmentskolonaki.gr*

Note: Long-stay suites and apartments are usually priced per month, but most offer weekly rates if requested

Left **Student and Travellers' Inn** Right **Athens International Youth Hostel**

TOP 10 Hostels, Camping & Cheap Sleeps

1 Pagration
Far from the sights of the city centre, but prices for dorm beds can't be beaten. This is the headquarters of the Greek Association of Youth Hostels, an organization that can help you find cheap accommodation throughout the country. ❧ *Damareos 75, Pangrati • 210 751 9530 • www. athensyhostel.com*

2 Fivos
Representing a great deal for its bulls-eye central location, Phivos is the newest city-centre addition to Athens' collection of hostels. The hostel is run by a very friendly and helpful owner, and all the rooms come with bathrooms and air conditioning. ❧ *Athinas 23, Monastiraki • Map J2 • 210 323 2455 • A/C • www.hotelfivos.gr*

3 Athens Backpackers
Set up by an Australian company, this hostel is located near Akropoli metro station and offers doubles, six- and eight-bed dorms and six- and four-bed apartments with cooking facilities. ❧ *Makri 12, Makrigianni • www.backpackers.gr*

4 Student and Travellers' Inn
This spotless, cheerful hostel is located in a pretty quarter of Plaka, an easy walk from most sights and downtown.

Private rooms and dorms have wooden floors, big windows and private phones with internet access. Bathrooms are shared, but each bedroom has its own sink. ❧ *Kydathinaion 16, Plaka • Map L4 210 324 4808 • A/C • www.student travellersinn.com*

5 Dioskouros Guest House
A favourite with the international backpacking set. Dorms and private rooms that sleep up to four are usually packed in summer, but students and young people don't seem to mind, instead enjoying the festive atmosphere. Most gather for a beer in the garden. ❧ *Pittakou 6, Plaka • Map L5 • 210 324 8165 • www.hotelfivos.gr*

6 Hotel Tempi
The best thing about the Tempi is its location on a central but quiet street, overlooking a church, the Monastiraki flower market and the Acropolis. Rooms are basic, but the family running the hotel are helpful and can arrange city tours. ❧ *Aiolou 29, Monas-tiraki • Map K3 • 210 321 3175 • www. tempihotel.gr*

7 Athens International Youth Hostel
The location is central, if a little seedy, but the super-cheap dorm beds are in immaculate, quiet rooms (fully renovated in

2006), and the staff are helpful. Facilities include laundry and a kitchen for guests. ❧ *Victor Hugo 16, Metaxourgio • Map B2 • 210 523 2540 • www. aiyh-victorhugo.com*

8 Zorba's Hotel
A good place for a night or two on a tight budget. Tiny, clean rooms and dorm beds on a noisy street in an area that's run down but close to the centre. Pluses are a welcoming staff who speak perfect English, and large bathrooms. ❧ *Gkilfordou 10, Omonia • Map C1 • 210 823 4239 • A/C • www. zorbashotel.com*

9 Hostel Aphrodite
Clean dorm beds and a lively atmosphere. Once again, a somewhat seedy area, but it's not too far to the centre and it's close to the train station. Facilities include laundry and pay internet access. Students and backpackers gather at the bar downstairs. ❧ *Einardou 12, Omonia • 210 881 0589 • Open Mar–Oct • www. hostelaphrodite.com*

10 Kokkino Limanaki Camping
A 40-minute drive northeast of the city centre, in the port town of Rafina, this campsite offers a seaside location with a beach, regular buses to Athens and ferries to several islands ❧ *Rafina • 210 360 2294 & 22940 31604 • www.athenscamping.com*

> ***Note:*** *All the establishments listed here are less than €50 per night; dorm beds are no more than €16 per night*

Left **Poseidon Resort** Centre **Nafplia Palace** Right **Xenia**

TOP 10 High-End Hotels Outside Athens

1 Grand Resort Lagonissi

This vast resort complex spreads out over its own peninsula between Sounio and Vouliagmeni. It encompasses 16 beaches, with a range of seafront suites and lavish villas with their own pools. There is also a host of restaurants and a variety of organized activities. ✆ *Athens–Sounio road, Lagonissi • Map T3 • 22910 76000 • www. lagonissiresort.gr • Apr–Nov • €€€€€*

2 Grecotel Cape Sounio

Besides all the mod cons you'd expect following a total overhaul, this branch of the Grecotel chain is set on a verdant hillside, with spectacular views of the sea and Temple of Poseidon. ✆ *Athens–Sounio Rd • Map T3 • 22920 69700 • www.grecotel.gr • €€€€*

3 Orloff Resort

This stylish boutique hotel is housed in a 19th-century mansion with an outdoor pool. The 19 rooms, studios and apartments incorporate traditional architecture with modern minimalist design. ✆ *Spetses • 22980 75444 • www.orloffresort. com • €€€*

4 Bratsera

This hotel in a former sponge factory is one of the most charming places to stay in all of Greece. The quaint rooms and flower-filled courtyard are lovely, and there's also an outdoor pool. ✆ *Harbour, Hydra • Map S4 • 22980 53971 • Mar–Oct • www. bratserahotel.com • €€€*

5 Poseidon Resort

This resort has a small private beach and extensive gardens, as well as sports, spa and conference facilities. Accommodation varies widely in size, style and luxury, from individual rooms to villas. The spruced-up bungalows are best, with their shiny wooden floors and cotton canopies. ✆ *Boutsi Loutrakiou area, Loutraki • Map R2 • 27440 67938 • www.poseidon resort.gr • €€€*

6 Nafplia Palace

Nafplio's nicest hotel now has a luxurious spa and beauty centre on the premises. New decorative touches include large, wood-and-marble rooms. What won't change, however, is its unbeatable location on the hill of Acronafplia, within the ancient fortress walls. ✆ *Acronafplia, Nafplio • Map R3 • 27520 70800 • www.nafplion hotels.gr • €€€*

7 AKS Porto Cheli

Overlooking the Argo-likos Gulf, this is a good base for exploring both the Peloponnese and the island of Spetses. It has 250 spacious rooms with large beds and offers a full range of resort services and activities, including childcare. ✆ *Portocheli • Map S4 • 2754 053 400 • www. akshotels.com • €€*

8 Thermae Sylla Grand Hotel

One of the best spas in Greece, the Thermae Sylla offers treatments in Evia's restorative mineral-laden spring waters, along with a wide array of beauty and relaxation treatments. The beautiful external architecture has been preserved, but rooms and treatment areas are fully modern. ✆ *Edipsos, Evia • Map S1 • 22260 60100 • www. thermaesylla.gr • €€€€*

9 Elatos Resort, Arachova

Greece's only Alpine resort is set in a pine forest at the edge of Parnassos National Park. All 40 chalets have two to three bedrooms, kitchens, fireplaces and verandas. The central buildings offer a fully equipped health club, bar and restaurant. ✆ *Itamos, nr Arachova • Map R1 • 22340 61162 • www.elatos.com • €€€€*

10 Delphi Palace

Comfortable, classic rooms with wooden accents have a wonderful view of the olive groves descending below Delphi. There is also an indoor pool and gym and fitness club. Pets are welcome. ✆ *Delphi • Map Q1 • 22650 82151 • www. delphi-hotels.gr • €€*

Note: *Unless otherwise stated, all hotels accept credit cards, have en-suite bathrooms and air conditioning (A/C)*

Price Categories

For a standard, double room per night (with breakfast if included), taxes and extra charges.

€	under €100
€€	€100–€150
€€€	€150–€250
€€€€	€250–€350
€€€€€	over €350

Hotel Parnassos

☂10 Mid & Budget Outside Athens

1 Hotel Ganimede
The rooms in this 19th-century mansion are simple but elegant; however, the real draw is the combination of a lovely courtyard garden overflowing with fragrant flowers, the sumptuous breakfasts and the warm hospitality of the Italian owners. ◈ *Gourgouri 16, Galaxidi • Map Q1 • 22650 41328 • www. ganimede.gr • €*

2 Archontiko
The themed rooms sound kitschy, but most manage to work. The "Bridal" has a huge canopy bed draped with sheer white linen; the "At Sea" is decorated like a boat; while adventurous couples go for the "Conception", with a round bed and mirrored ceiling. When not enjoying their rooms, guests can stroll in the pleasant garden. ◈ *Visithra, close to the harbour, Galaxidi • Map Q1 • 22650 42292 • No credit cards • €*

3 Hotel Belle Helene
German archaeologist Heinrich Schliemann slept here (room No. 3) while excavating Mycenae, and many a classicist has followed in his footsteps. Modern tourists can enjoy clean, quiet, comfortable rooms in addition to the hotel's interesting historic cachet. ◈ *Christou Tsounta 15, Mycenae • Map R3 • 27510 76225 • €*

4 Pension Acronafplla
If this pretty pension is full, the owners can find rooms for you in one of their other small hotels around town. Within the pension, the accommodation varies – not all rooms have private bathrooms or air conditioning, but the pricing reflects this fairly. Many options are very pleasant, including rooms with colourfully painted wooden floors and wrought-iron beds. ◈ *Vasileos Konstandinou 23, Nafplio • Map R3 • 27520 24481 • www.pension-acronafplia.com • €*

5 Dimitris Bekas
The best budget option in Nafplio. These rooms in the old city are plain and spare, but clean, and there's a great sea view from the sitting area on the roof. All rooms have televisions, but most share a bathroom. No A/C, but fans and the high location keep things cool. ◈ *Efthimiopoulou 26, Nafplio • Map R3 • 27520 24594 • No A/C or credit cards • €*

6 King Othon
This two-storey Neo-Classical building with delightfully painted ceilings is located near the centre of old Nafplio. Rooms come in several sizes, and breakfast includes home-baked goodies. ◈ *Farmakopoulou 4, Nafplio • Map R3 • 27520 27595 • www. kingothon.gr • €*

7 Hotel Tholos
This is a good budget option in Delphi. Rooms are cheap, clean and nicely furnished, and the owners are friendly. ◈ *Apollonos 31, Delphi • Map Q1 • 22650 82268 • No A/C or credit cards • €*

8 Hotel Olympic
A slightly more up-market, but still very affordable, Delphi option. Rooms are cosy, rustic and clean, and the fireplace in the lounge feels great during winters. ◈ *Vasileon Pavlou & Frideriks 59, Delphi • Map Q1 • 2265 082793 • www. olympic-hotel.gr • €*

9 Hotel Parnassos
A good budget option just outside the mountain village of Arachova. There is one bathroom for every two of the spare but clean rooms. No A/C, but Mount Parnassos rarely gets hot enough to need it. ◈ *Delphon, Arachova • Map R1 • 22670 31307 • No A/C • €*

10 Eginitiko Arhontiko
A 19th-century mansion with loads of character: painted ceilings, a stained-glass-windowed parlour and a garden courtyard. Rooms are small and clean, albeit with a few peeling paint patches here and there and banging pipes. ◈ *Thomaidou & Agios Nikoloau, Agia Marina, Aegina • Map S3 • 22970 24968 • €*

General Index

Index

Index

Acknowledgements

The Authors
Coral Davenport and Jane Foster are free-lance travel and features writers, based in Athens. Additional text on shopping and entertainment was provided by a fellow Athens-based writer, Cordelia Madden.

Produced by BLUE ISLAND PUBLISHING, LONDON www.blueisland.co.uk

Editorial Director
Rosalyn Thiro
Art Director
Stephen Dero
Associate Editor
Michael Ellis
Picture Research
Ellen Root
Proofread and indexed by
Jane Simmonds
Main Photographer
Nigel Hicks
Additional Photography:
Joe Cornish, Rupert Horrox, Rob Reichenfeld, Clive Streeter, Peter Wilson
Cartography
John Plumer

AT DORLING KINDERSLEY

Series Publisher
Douglas Amrine
Publishing Manager
Fay Franklin, Kate Poole
Senior Art Editor
Marisa Renzullo
Cartographic Editor
Casper Morris
DTP
Jason Little, Conrad van Dyk
Production
Sarah Dodd
Design & Editorial Assistance
Jane Foster, Anna Freiberger, Juliet Kenny, Quadrum Solutions, Pete Quinlan

PHOTOGRAPHY PERMISSIONS: Dorling Kindersley would like to thank all the churches, museums, hotels, restaurants, bars, clubs, shops, galleries and other sights for their assistance and kind permission to photograph at their establishments.

Placement Key: t = top; tl = top left; tr = top right; tc = top centre; c = centre; cl + center left; cr = center right; b = bottom; bl = bottom left; d = detail.

48 THE RESTAURANT: 57tl; 4CORNERS IMAGES: SIME/Biscaro Alberto 11br

AKG, LONDON: 34tl/tr, 35l, 35r, 36tl(d), 37tl(d), 38tc; Cameraphoto 38tl; John Hios 36c, 37c(d); Erich Lessing 36b, 36tc, 36tr(d), 38b, 38tr, 39t(d)/c/b(d), 61; ALAMY IMAGES: EuroStock 46tl.

BENAKI MUSEUM: M Skiadaresis 2tc, 22c/b, 23t/cl/cr/b, BERNARD TSCHUMI ARCHITECTS: 11c; BRASIL HOTEL APART-MENTS:144tl; BRIDGEMAN ART LIBRARY: Acropolis Museum, Athens 40tl; Fitzwilliam Musuem, University of Cambridge, UK 40tr; Musee Municipal Antoine Vivenel, Compiegne, France 40c; National Archaeological Museum, Athens, Greece 64c; BYZANTINE MUSEUM: 29tl, 29tr.

CALLIRHOE HOTEL: 141tl; Courtesy of the CITY OF ATHENS MUSEUM: 87b; CORBIS: Hulton Deutsch Collection 64tr; Gianni Dagli Orti 16c, 41t.

Courtesy of the HELLENIC FESTIVAL SA: 00b(d).

Courtesy of the JEWISH MUSEUM OF GREECE: 72tr.

Courtesy of KAZANTAKIS PUBLICATIONS: 37b(d); KOBAL COLLECTION: 20th Century Fox 65bl.

METROPOLITAN HOTEL: 141tr.

NICHOLAS P GOULANDRIS FOUNDATION MUSEUM OF CYCLADIC AND ANCIENT GREEK ART: 18–9l all; 42c.

ORGANISING COMMITTEE FOR THE OLYMPIC GAMES ATHENS 2004: 62tc/62tr.

PHOTOSTOCK, Athens: 15c, 29c, 29t, 60c, 64tl; PLOUS PODILATOU: 106tc.

ROBERTHARDING.COM: Tony Gervis 60tr.

VENUE BAR: 85tl.

Phrase Book

In an Emergency

Help!	**Voítheia!**	vo-ee-theea!
Stop!	**Stamatíste!**	sta-ma-tee-steh!
Call a doctor!	**Fonáxte éna giatró!**	fo-nak-steh ! e-na ya-tro!
Call an ambulance/	**Kaléste to asthenofóro/tin**	ka-le-steh to as-the-no-fo-ro teen a-sti-no-the
the police/ fire brigade!	**astynomía/tin pyrosvestikí!**	mía/teen pee-ro-zve-stee-kee!
Where is the nearest telephone/ hospital/ pharmacy?	**Poú eínai to plisiéstero tiléfono/ nosokomeío/ farmakeío?**	poo ee-ne to plee-see-e-ste-ro tee-le-pho-no/no-so-ko-mee-o/far-ma-kee-o?

Communication Essentials

Yes	**Nai**	neh
No	**Ochi**	o-chee
Please	**Parakaló**	pa-ra-ka-lo
Thank you	**Efcharistó**	ef-cha-ree-sto
You are welcome	**Parakaló**	pa-ra-ka-lo
OK/alright	**Entáxei**	en-dak-zee
Excuse me	**Me synchoreíte**	me seen-cho-ree-teh
Hello	**Geiá sas**	yeea sas
Goodbye	**Antío**	an-dee-o
Good morning	**Kaliméra**	ka-lee-me-ra
Good night	**Kalin'ychta**	ka-lee-neech-ta
Morning	**Proí**	pro-ee
Afternoon	**Apógevma**	a-po-yev-ma
Evening	**Vrádi**	vrath-i
This morning	**Símera to proí**	see-me-ra to pro-ee
Yesterday	**Chthés**	chthes
Today	**Símera**	see-me-ra
Tomorrow	**Avrio**	av-ree-o
Here	**Edó**	ed-o
There	**Ekeí**	e-kee
What?	**Tí?**	tee?
Why?	**Giatí?**	ya-tee?
Where?	**Poú?**	poo?
How?	**Pós?**	pos?
Wait!	**Perímene!**	pe-ree-me-neh!
How are you?	**Tí káneis?**	tee ka-nees?
Very well, thank you.	**Poly kalá, efcharistó.**	po-lee ka-la, ef-cha-ree-sto.
How do you do?	**Pós eíste?**	pos ees-te?

Pleased to meet you.	**Chaíro pol'y.**	che-ro po-lee.
What is your name?	**Pós légeste?**	pos le-ye-ste?
Where is/are...?	**Poú eínai...?**	poo ee-ne...?
How far is it to...?	**Póso apéchei...?**	po-so a-pe-chee?
How do I get to...?	**Pós mporó na páo...?**	pos bo-ro-na pa-o...?
Do you speak English?	**Miláte Angliká?**	mee-la-te an-glee-ka?
I understand.	**Katalavaíno.**	ka-ta-la-ve-no.
I don't understand.	**Den katalavaíno.**	then ka-ta-la-ve-no.
Could you speak slowly?	**Miláte lígo pio argá parakaló?**	mee-la-te lee-go pyo ar-ga pa-ra-ka-lo?
I'm sorry.	**Me synchoreíte.**	me seen-cho-ree teh.
Does anyone have a key?	**Echei kanénas kleidí?**	e-chee ka-ne-nas klee-dee?

Useful Words

big	**Megálo**	me-ga-lo
small	**Mikró**	mi-kro
hot	**Zestó**	zes-to
cold	**Kr'yo**	kree-o
good	**Kaló**	ka-lo
bad	**Kakó**	ka-ko
enough	**Arketá**	ar-ke-ta
well	**Kalá**	ka-la
open	**Anoichtá**	a-neech-ta
closed	**Kleistá**	klee-sta
left	**Aristerá**	a-ree-ste-ra
right	**Dexiá**	dek-see-a
straight on	**Eftheía**	ef-thee-a
between	**Anámesa / Metax'y**	a-na-me-sa/me-tak-see
on the corner of..	**Sti gonía tou...**	stee go-nee-a too
near	**Kontá**	kon-da
far	**Makriá**	ma-kree-a
up	**Epáno**	e-pa-no
down	**Káto**	ka-to
early	**Norís**	no-rees
late	**Argá**	ar-ga
entrance	**I eísodos**	ee ee-so-thos
exit	**I éxodos**	ee e-kso-dos
toilet occupied/ engaged	**Oi toualétes / Kateiliméni**	ee-too-a-le-tes ka-tee-lee-me-nee

Note: words in bold (centre columns) are transliterated according to the system used by the Greek Government. However, this system is not used consistently throughout Greece, and visitors will encounter many variants on road signs, menus etc.

unoccupied	**Eléftheri**	e-lef-the-ree
free/no charge	**Doreán**	tho-re-**an**
in/out	**Mésa/ Exo**	me-sa/**e**k-so

Making a Telephone Call

Where is the nearest public telephone?	**Poú vrísketai o plisiésteros tilefonikós thálamos?**	poo vree**s**-ke-teh o plee-see-**e**-ste-ros tee-le-fo-ni-**ko**s tha-**la**-mos?
I would like to place a long-distance call.	**Tha íthela na káno éna yperastikó tilefónima.**	tha ee-the-la na ka-no **e**-na ee-pe-ra-sti-**ko** tee-le-**fo**-nee-ma.
I would like to reverse the charges.	**Tha íthela na chreóso to tilefónima ston paralípti.**	tha e-the-la na chre-**o**-so to tee-le-**fo**-nee-ma ston pa-ra-lep-tee.
I will try again later.	**Tha xanatilefoníso argótera.**	tha ksa-na-tee-le-fo-ni-so ar-**go**-te-ra.
Can I leave a message?	**Mporeíte na tou afísete éna mínyma?**	bo-ree-te na too a-fee-se-teh e-na mee-nee-ma?
Could you speak up a little please?	**Miláte dynatótera, parakaló?**	mee **la**-teh dee-na-to-te-ra, pa-ra-ka-**lo**?
Hold on.	**Periménete.**	pe-ri me-ne-teh.
local call	**Topikó tilefónima**	to-pi-ko tee-le-fo-nee-ma
OTE telephone office	**O OTE / To tilefoneío**	o O-**TE** / To tee-le-fo-ne-**o**
phone box/kiosk	**O tilefonikós thálamos**	o tee-le-fo-ni-**ko**s tha-**la**-mos
phone card	**I tilekárta**	ee tee-le-**ka**r-ta

Shopping

How much does this cost?	**Póso kánei?**	po-so **ka**-nee?
I would like.....	**Tha íthela...**	tha ee-the-la...
Do you have......?	**Échete...?**	**e**-rhe-teh...?
I am just looking.	**Aplós koitáo.**	a-plos kee-ta-o.
Do you take credit cards/ travellers' cheques?	**travellers' cheques Décheste pistotikés kártes/ travellers' cheques?**	the-ches-teh pee-sto-tee-kes kar-tes/ travellers' cheques?
What time do you open/close?	**Póte anoígete/ kleínete?**	po-teh a-nee-ye-teh/ klee-ne-teh?
Can you ship this overseas?	**Mporeíte na to steílete sto exoterikó?**	bo-ree-teh na to stee-le-teh sto e-xo-te-ree ko?

This one.	**Aftó edó.**	af-to e-do.
That one.	**Ekeíno.**	e-kee-no.
expensive	**Akrivó**	a-kree-vo
cheap	**Fthinó**	fthee-no
size	**To mégethos**	to me-ge-thos
white	**Lefkó**	lef-ko
black	**Mávro**	mav-ro
red	**Kókkino**	ko-kee-no
yellow	**Kítrino**	kee-tree-no
green	**Prásino**	pra-see-no
blue	**Mple**	bleh

Types of Shop

antique shop	**Magazí me antíkes**	ma-ga-zee-me an-dee-kes
bakery	**O foúrnos**	o foor-nos
bank	**I trápeza**	ee tra-pe-za
bazaar	**To pazári**	to pa-za-ree
bookshop	**To vivliopoleío**	to vee-vlee-o-po-lee-o
butcher	**To kreopoleío**	to kre-o-po-lee-o
cake shop	**To zacharo-plasteío**	to za-cha-ro-pla-stee-o
cheese shop	**Magazí me allantiká**	ma-ga-zee me a-lan-dee-ka
department store	**Polykatástima**	Po-lee ka-**ta**-stee-ma
fishmarket	**To ichthyopoleío/ psarádiko**	to eech-thee-o-po-lee-o /psa-rá-dee-ko
greengrocer	**To manáviko**	ma-na-vee-ko
hairdresser	**To kommotírio**	to ko-mo-tee ree-o
kiosk	**To períptero**	to pe-reep-te-ro
leather shop	**Magazí me dermátina eídi**	ma-ga-zee me ther-ma-tee-na ee-thee
street market	**I laïkí agorá**	ee la-ee-kee a-go-ra
newsagent	**O efimeridopólis**	O e-fee-me-ree-tho-po-lees
pharmacy	**To farmakeío**	to far-ma-kee-o
post office	**To tachydromeío**	to ta-chee-thro-mee-o
shoe shop	**Katástima y podimáton**	ka-ta-stee-ma ee-po-dee-ma-ton
souvenir shop	**Magazí me "souvenir"**	ma-ga-zee meh "souvenir"
supermarket	**"Supermarket" / Yperagorá**	"Supermarket" / ee-per-a-go-ra

Bold letters in the pronunciation guides (right columns) indicate the stressed syllable.

English	Greek (transliterated)	Pronunciation
tobacconist	**Eídi kapnistoú**	Ee-thee kap-nees
travel agent	**To taxeidiotikó grafeío**	to tak-see-thy-o-tee-ko gra-fee-o

Sightseeing

English	Greek (transliterated)	Pronunciation
tourist information	**O EOT**	o E-OT
tourist police	**I touristikí astynomía**	ee too-rees-tee-kee a-stee-no-mee-a
archaeological	**archaiologikós**	ar-che-o-lo-yee-kos
art gallery	**I gkalerí**	ee ga-le-ree
beach	**I paralía**	ee pa-ra-lee-a
Byzantine	**vyzantinós**	vee-zan-dee-nos
castle	**To kástro**	to ka-stro
cathedral	**I mitrópoli**	ee mee-tro-po-lee
cave	**To spílaio**	to spee-le-o
church	**I ekklisía**	ee e-klee-see-a
folk art	**laïkí téchni**	la-ee-kee tech-nee
fountain	**To syntriváni**	to seen-dree-va-nee
hill	**O lófos**	o lo-fos
historical	**istorikós**	ee-sto-ree-kos
island	**To nisí**	to nee-see
lake	**I límni**	ee leem-nee
library	**I vivliothíki**	ee veev-lee-o-thee-kee
mansion	**I épavlis**	ee e-pav-lees
monastery	**moní**	mo-ni
mountain	**To vounó**	to voo-no
municipal	**dimotikós**	thee-mo-tee-kos
museum	**To mouseío**	to moo-see-o
national	**ethnikós**	eth-nee-kos
park	**To párko**	to par-ko
garden	**O kípos**	o kee-pos
gorge	**To farángi**	to fa-ran-gee
grave of....	**O táfos tou...**	o ta-fos too
river	**To potámi**	to po-ta-mee
road	**O drómos**	o thro-mos
saint	**ágios/ágioi/ agía/agíes**	a-yee-os/a-yee-ee/a-yee-a/a-yee-es
spring	**I pigí**	ee pee-yee
square	**I plateía**	ee pla-tee-a
stadium	**To stádio**	to sta-thee-o
statue	**To ágalma**	to a-gal-ma
theatre	**To théatro**	to the-a-tro
town hall	**To dimarcheío**	to thee-mar-chee-o
closed on public holidays	**kleistó tis argíes**	klee-sto tees aryee-es

Transport

English	Greek (transliterated)	Pronunciation
When does the .... leave?	**Póte févgei to...?**	po-teh fev-yee to...?
Where is the bus stop?	**Poú eínai i stási tou leoforeíou?**	poo ee-neh ee sta-see too le-o-fo-ree-oo...?
Is there a bus to..?	**Ypárchei leoforeío gia...?**	ee-par-chee le-o-fo-ree-o yia...?
ticket office	**Ekdotíria eisitiríon**	Ek-tho-tee-reea ee-see-tee-ree-on
return ticket	**Eisitírio me epistrofí**	ee-see-tee-ree-o meh e-pee-stro-fee
single journey	**Apló eisitírio**	a-plo ee-see-tee-reeo
bus station	**O stathmós leoforeíon**	o stath-mos leo-fo-ree-on
bus ticket	**Eisitírio leoforeíou**	ee-see-tee-ree-o leo-fo-ree-oo
trolley bus	**To trólley**	to tro-le-ee
port	**To limán**	to lee-ma-nee
train/metro	**To tréno**	to tre-no
railway station	**sidirodromikós stathmós**	see-thee-ro-thro-mee-kos stath-mos
moped	**To motopodílato/ To michanáki**	to mo-to-po-thee-la-to/to mee-cha-na-kee
bicycle	**To podílato**	to po-thee-la-to
taxi	**To taxí**	to tak-see
airport	**To aerodrómio**	to a-e-ro-thro-mee-o
ferry	**To "ferry-boat"**	to fe-ree-bot
hydrofoil	**To delfíni / To ydroptérygo**	to del-fee-nee / To ee-throp-te-ree-go
catamaran	**To katamarán**	to catamaran
for hire	**Enoikiázontai**	e-nee-kya-zon-deh

Note: words in bold (centre columns) are transliterated according to the system used by the Greek Government. However, this system is not used consistently throughout Greece, and visitors will encounter many variants on road signs, menus etc.